STAGE 5:

A CANCER JOURNEY

Also By David Chill

Post Pattern

Fade Route

Bubble Screen

Safety Valve

Corner Blitz

Nickel Package

Double Pass

Tampa Two

Flea Flicker

Swim Move

Hard Count

Jet Sweep

Bull Rush

Curse Of The Afflicted

STAGE 5:

A CANCER JOURNEY

David Chill

ISBN 978-1-7353230-1-5

This book is a memoir. It reflects the author's present recollections of his experiences over time. In some instances, events have been compressed and dialogue has been re-created. The names and identifying characteristics of some persons described in the book have been changed.

For Dr. Daniel Lieber

Author's Note

A few years ago I came across a quote, written in chalk, but later attributed to Brené Brown, the professor at the University of Texas. It simply said: "One day you will tell your story of how you overcame what you went through, and it will be someone else's survival guide."

This is my story. My wish in writing this book is that it will help others to create a path forward. At the very least, it can provide something else. It can provide hope.

Contents

1

A Pain In The Back

In March 2012, I was diagnosed with stage 4 lung cancer. It is a terminal illness. There is no cure.

Stage 4 is considered the final stage. My life expectancy was described in months, not years. I knew precious little about cancer, but I did know I had to act on it. Cancer moves quickly. I was 55 years old and death was suddenly staring me in the face.

Up until that point, I thought I was in excellent health. I thought I had good genes. My father lived until age 86, and my mother was still alive at 88. I was fit, I walked 10 miles a week, and I was a moderate drinker. Except for inhaling some weed during college, I was a non-smoker. And even though we lived in Los Angeles, we were near the beach and the coastal air was clean. I had every reason to believe I would live as long as my parents. Maybe longer.

A few weeks before my diagnosis, I began to experience pain in my back when I breathed deeply. I shrugged it off as a minor annoyance that would soon go away, just as many small aches and pains go away. Maybe I pulled a muscle at the gym. Maybe it was a lingering issue from a recent cold. It could have been anything. After a few weeks though, my wife suggested I go see the doctor, and she soon began to suggest it more forcefully.

There's a reason why married men live longer than unmarried men, and it has little to do with warm companionship or regular sex. After her suggestions led to insistence, I finally caved. From my days of working at Disney, I knew about the nag factor. Nagging works on parents, and it also works on spouses. It spurs action. I set up an appointment with Dr. Earl Gordon, our family physician.

Earl Gordon is literally a doctor's doctor. Many years earlier, I'd become disenchanted with my primary care physician. A podiatrist I was seeing for a foot injury recommended Dr. Gordon. The podiatrist told me that all of the doctors in his office saw Earl. There is no better sign of a good doctor than when other doctors go see him themselves. They are more informed. They have insider knowledge.

I set up a lunchtime appointment at Dr. Gordon's office in Santa Monica, which was not very convenient to where I worked in El Segundo, a good half-hour drive. But the appointment time fit nicely into my day.

I was working as a marketing research executive at DirecTV and normally had a busy schedule. In addition to having a demanding career, I was married, we had a son who was 13 years old, and we had an active social calendar. Life was good.

After Dr. Gordon examined me, I expected him to refer me to an orthopedist who specialized in back issues. Instead, he asked me to go in for a chest X-ray. There was an imaging center nearby, and he could set something up right away. I checked my afternoon meetings and saw that I didn't have anything until later in the day. It was an uneventful Tuesday. My calendar was open, so I shrugged and said okay, but I could have just as easily put it off to a later date. That simple, innocuous decision could have been tragic. I strolled a few blocks to the imaging center. It was a sunny day, and I enjoyed my walk past the old bungalows and cottages that dot the Santa Monica landscape. The process did not take long. I had the chest X-ray and then drove back to my office.

At about 4:30 p.m., Dr. Gordon called me. His voice resonated with a deep baritone, but he seemed calm and thoughtful. I was surprised to receive his call; after returning to the office I had buried myself in work, and had largely forgotten about the X-ray.

"I have to tell you something," he said, not mincing words. "We found a small mass on your left lung."

At that moment, my world changed. I did not know much about having a mass on the lung, but I did know it was often related to lung cancer. My mother-in-law had passed away from the disease a few years earlier, but she had been a frequent smoker when she was young. I believed, as many people believe, that lung cancer just affects smokers. As I would soon learn, as many as 20 percent of lung cancer patients are non-smokers.

"Could this be benign?" I asked, depleting a good portion of my knowledge of cancer in that one sentence.

"We don't know that," he answered. "But it's worrisome."

Dr. Gordon wanted to move quickly, and he scheduled me for a PET scan and a CT scan over the next few days. These are tests designed to identify if cancer might exist in the body, where the cancer could be located, and how large any tumors might be. It is an inexact science. Scans record images of the body at different angles; they can provide detailed insights that are far greater than an ordinary X-ray can. They don't provide iron-clad proof that a person actually has cancer. They are pictures. But they can tell quite a story.

I went through being scanned in a bit of a daze. I was caught completely off-guard. I had no plan, and I had no clear sense of what to do. I talked to my wife, Andrea, but I was nowhere near ready to discuss any of this with our son, Matthew, who was fortunately away on a class trip that week. And realistically, it might turn out to be nothing, and there was no need to alarm anyone, much less a child, until we knew exactly what this was.

Dr. Gordon called me after the scans and said he wanted me to go see a respiratory specialist. I didn't ask him for the results, and he didn't volunteer. Maybe I was in too much shock to be thinking clearly.

And maybe I just didn't want to know the answer.

2

Diagnosis: Stage 4

The respiratory specialist was Dr. Wellington, a pleasant doctor, who told me they would drain the fluid that had built up in my lung. This was a minor in-office procedure called a thoracentesis, and it would provide some relief for the discomfort in my back. They would send this fluid to a lab, where it would be tested to determine if it was cancerous. He encouraged me to look into having a procedure called a pleurodesis, which uses talc to bond the space in the chest, keeping fluid from building up in the future.

While his technician drained the fluid, I noticed it had an odd ruddy color, a light reddish-brown hue that reminded me of apple cider. The process took a few minutes, and I looked around the exam room. It had the typical white walls and utilitarian furnishings, but I noticed a poster on the back of the door detailing the stages of lung cancer. I did not understand why he would put up this poster. I also did not understand how someone like me, a non-smoker in seemingly good health, could possibly get this disease. Aside from the pain in my back, I had no other symptoms. I mostly felt fine. The whole episode felt surreal, as if I was starring in someone else's horror movie.

My visit to Dr. Wellington was on a Friday, and he told me he would have results early the following week. I mentioned that we were about to leave for a driving vacation through Arizona, and he said he would call me with the results. It was our son's spring break, and we had planned to spend a day or two in Phoenix, drive through Sedona, hike for a few days around the Grand Canyon, and then do a one-night stopover in Las Vegas. A short break from the day-to-day grind of modern life.

Before we left on our trip, I did what doctors advise patients not to do – I went online to seek information. The reason is that some of the information on the Web could be incorrect or outdated, or just complete nonsense. I read that someone was trying to prove that dogs could smell cancer on a person's breath. Another told of how brightly colored vegetables could cure any malady. From laetrile to coffee enemas, there was a long list of cures for cancer, and many seemed spurious, if not outright absurd.

I also learned about a cancer treatment, one supposedly developed by a German scientist who had been nominated for a Nobel Prize. The protocol included eating a mixture of flaxseed oil and cottage cheese. Since this seemed like a concoction that, at the very least, could do no harm, I tried it. This mixture turned out to be vile; I could only swallow it after a generous sprinkling of cayenne pepper was able to mask the taste.

Further research informed me that absolutely anyone could be nominated for a Nobel Prize, and that on a scale of noteworthy accomplishments, it was a low bar to clear. I also learned that this scientist's theories had been debunked many years ago, and were often associated with the word quackery. There was zero legitimate evidence this, or any diet, could cure cancer. The only thing many people seemed to agree on was that the taste was nasty, and this diet would not be a cure for anything.

Still, the internet did give me some nuggets of information that seemed credible. When fluid drained from the lung has a ruddy, reddish-brown color, it is very often a sign that the fluid contains malignancies. This can indicate a stage 4 cancer diagnosis, meaning the disease was terminal. Another website provided an even more dire indicator: lung cancer patients who were at this stage had a 5-year survival rate of less than 10 percent. The flip side of this is 90 percent of stage 4 lung cancer patients die within 5 years. I did not know what stage I was actually in, but this information was clearly sobering. I confirmed all this on a few other websites, and I finally understood that the remainder of my life could be very short. There is no good way to process that. It is a body blow.

Lung cancer is the deadliest of all cancers, meaning that more people die of lung cancer than any other type of cancer. I learned that 1 out of 16 people in America will be diagnosed with lung cancer in their lifetime. It does not distinguish by gender; roughly half of those diagnosed are men, and half are women. The good news was lung cancer was declining in America, as fewer people smoked cigarettes. The bad news happened only if you got it. And worse, I learned that many of those who are diagnosed with lung cancer do not find out until the cancer is in the late stages. It often moves silently.

We left for Arizona the following Monday. I called Dr. Wellington multiple times over the next two days and none of my calls were returned. As someone who believes it is better to know the reality of a situation than to not know, this lack of communication was disturbing. It only added to my stress.

Frustrated, I finally called Dr. Gordon and asked if he could find lab results from the testing of the fluid they drained from my lung. He called back an hour later. They had found malignancies. That, combined with my scan results, confirmed I had lung cancer. He told me he would set up an appointment the following week with a highly respected oncologist, Dr. Daniel Lieber, who would take me through treatment options. Dr. Lieber was not a lung cancer specialist, but rather an excellent doctor who worked tirelessly for his patients. Dr. Gordon described him as obsessive. He said I'd be in good hands.

The rest of the day was a blur. We visited an aquarium that afternoon and went back to our hotel to use the pool. Our wedding anniversary had been a few days before, and the three of us went to a nice restaurant in Scottsdale to celebrate, but I was hardly good company. I discreetly told Andrea about my call with Dr. Gordon, but I was in no way ready to discuss this with Matthew. I could barely process it myself. All I remember about the restaurant was that it was dark and quiet.

The next day, we drove north toward the Grand Canyon and stopped for lunch at a wonderful spot in Sedona called the Enchantment Resort. I was still rolling things over in my mind, but a good night's sleep, with the aid of a few beers, seemed to help. I did not know a lot about lung cancer at the time, and that might have been a good thing. Ignorance is bliss.

We enjoyed cheeseburgers at the Enchantment, and had a gorgeous view of the distant red rocks that Sedona is famous for. Below us, a bright blue pool shimmered, and I started to feel a little better. Pretty surroundings help. We took a walk around the resort, and finally left to make our way toward the Grand Canyon. But a few minutes into our drive, my cell phone rang. I saw it was Dr. Wellington calling. I pulled into an empty parking lot, which, ironically belonged to the Solid Rock Church of Sedona.

I jumped out of the car and began to speak with him, as I walked aimlessly around the asphalt lot. A number of weeds had sprung up on the pavement. He found out I had called Dr. Gordon, and he apologized for not getting back to me. He said he didn't want to spoil our family vacation by providing bad news. I didn't tell him the anxiety of not knowing was already spoiling the vacation, but I did ask him a question I had forgotten to ask Dr. Gordon.

"What stage am I in?" I asked, tepidly.

"This would be stage 4," he replied, not showing any hesitation.

"Oh, my God," I blurted out, almost involuntarily. It was the last stage. It meant the cancer had spread to other parts of the body, which also meant it could not be removed through either surgery or radiation. Dr. Wellington, sensing my dismay, then tried to reassure me.

"You know," he told me, "there are a lot of new treatments being developed now for lung cancer. I happen to know a number of patients who have been living with lung cancer for three years now."

Three years.

That comment would stay with me forever. I was 55, and had every reason to believe I would live a long life. But the world throws you curveballs. Within one week, this belief in my longevity had been shattered, blown to smithereens. Good eating habits, regular exercise, minimizing vices, none of these had done any good. I would not live another three decades, but with a little luck, I might live another three years. Dr. Wellington had wanted to be encouraging. He tried to reassure me. But in the end, he wound up doing the opposite. I felt crushed.

I thanked Dr. Wellington for finally calling me back. I hung up, and never spoke with him again.

3

Brushes With Death

It was not until I reached age 16 that I experienced the death of a loved one. My grandfather passed away after a lengthy illness, but he was in his 80s, and he had lived a long life. I had been spared from death for many years, but no one is spared indefinitely, and my next experience was truly jarring. I was 19 years old, and home from college for winter break. As a student, I had become something of a night owl, and I was watching TV at 12:30 a.m. when the phone rang. My parents were asleep. I assumed it was a call from a friend. It was, rather, a call from the Wyoming Highway Patrol, and the officer specifically asked to speak with me.

A few years earlier, my older brother, Jeffrey, had moved from our home in New York City to Laramie, close to the University of Wyoming. He wanted to live in a college town, and he wanted to open a karate school. He had a tough go of making the school profitable, and took odd jobs as a short-order cook and a delivery truck driver. Eventually, he met a girl there and they fell in love. That Christmas, he was supposed to have come back to New York for a few days to spend time with our family. Instead, he chose to take a driving trip with his girlfriend, up to Montana.

What happened that night remains a mystery. The roads were clear and the weather was good, albeit bitter cold. But my brother, in an old Volkswagen Beetle, got into a head-on collision with a large sedan. Jeffrey and his girlfriend were killed upon impact; the other driver sustained only minor injuries. The other driver claimed Jeffrey's Volkswagen had crossed the double yellow line, and he was unable to react quickly enough to avoid a collision. There were no witnesses; his version of events was the only one available.

"I'm sorry to inform you of this," the officer had said, "but your brother and his girlfriend were involved in an auto accident tonight. We transported them to the hospital, but they didn't make it. Now, I'm going to need your help here."

The officer continued speaking, but I didn't hear another word. I was in shock. One moment a person is with us, and the next moment they are gone. I did not get to say goodbye to my brother. He was 24 years old, and he would always be 24. His life froze at that moment. His death was sudden and unexpected and tragic.

We had few details. In a morbid twist, we received a letter from him the next afternoon, written a few days earlier, explaining that he had changed his mind at the last moment, about coming to New York. In fact, he had written this letter while at the airport to catch his flight. It was when his flight was boarding that he decided to remain in Wyoming, and take the fateful drive to Montana. Life turned dramatically on a whim, a decision that should not have had life-altering consequences. But it did, Jeffrey was suddenly gone, and our family was left to pick up the pieces and try to make sense of it all.

It is often said that parents never recover from the loss of a child. It is not how the world is supposed to work. Children bury their parents, hopefully after they've had a long and fruitful life. When a parent has to bury a child, they often bury a part of themselves as well. The only thing that can help ease the anguish is time, putting distance between the life they once had and the devastation that comes with death. And while my father was able to compartmentalize this and move on, I don't think my mother ever fully did. She did her best to put on a good face, but a whiff of sadness would remain with her forever.

One of the curious things about mourning the loss of a loved one is that you notice life still goes on around you. There is the funeral, the mourning period, the relatives coming together to help ease the grief. But you also see others going about their lives, and soon you have to join them. At one point, a few months later, my mother commented that it seemed as if Jeffrey had been forgotten, as if his existence had been relegated to a small and distant place, one where he would stay forever.

There had been countless trees planted in his name, donations made to charities, but slowly, only our memories of him remained. We struggled with this for years, trying to find a healing mechanism. My mother had always done the best she could for us, but there wasn't a lot I could do to help her, other than by talking with her and trying to guide her through the mourning process. I'm not sure how good I was at this; I was 19 and could barely help myself get through it.

After college, I headed to Los Angeles and enrolled in graduate school at the University of Southern California. Shortly thereafter, my parents took early retirement and moved an hour north of New York City to a small, rural town called Hopewell Junction. In the end, time and distance really seemed to be the best way to heal. It was not perfect, but neither was wallowing in grief. Loved ones die; you learn to live with this.

My relationship with my father was different, and our interactions were difficult ones. He liked to think of himself as a tough disciplinarian, his goal being to have his two sons grow up with the ability to handle whatever ill fate the world threw at them. He gave us praise in small and measured doses. Life had been hard for him, and he expected it would be hard for us. Maybe he was successful in toughening us up, but he also created a desire in both Jeffrey and myself to move far away, as soon as we had the opportunity.

I think my father came to regret having employed this tactic, especially after Jeffrey's death. He tried to become closer with me, but he didn't really know how, and our adult relationship was always formal and stiff and distant. In later years, he was stricken with Alzheimer's disease, and there is a school of thought that says people who develop dementia often do so because they do not want to recall the agony they encountered in their lives. The simple act of forgetting their memories allows them a level of peace. I think he managed to do that. When he died in June 2000, he reached a point where he was completely unaware of who I was.

Death is not something we typically think about when we're young, or even when we're middle-aged. It is with good reason. Pondering the end of life is a difficult thing to do, it can be painful to consider, and it's confusing as well. At my mother-in-law's funeral in 2008, I recalled walking through the cemetery and looking at some of the gravestones. There were plenty of people who lived into their 80s and 90s, but also a surprising number who passed away in their 50s. They couldn't all have been in car accidents. Be it cancer, heart disease, or other maladies, not everyone gets to lead a full life. I didn't know it then, but in a few short years, I would be facing a similar predicament. And even though I had tried to lead a healthy lifestyle, those efforts would be thwarted by the biggest impediment of all. Bad luck.

I had had a brush with death once, although not in the type of dramatic way one often thinks of. In 1995, I took a plane trip to watch USC play a football game against Penn State. There were no direct flights from Los Angeles to Pittsburgh, so I needed to change planes in Chicago. Two airlines, United and US Air, both offered flights at similar times, and the prices were about the same. I chose United, mostly because I had more miles in their frequent flier program, but if the other flight had been cheaper, I might well have chosen US Air.

When I arrived in Pittsburgh, my friend, Rick DeLoia, picked me up at the airport. He was white as a sheet, and told me how relieved he was to see me. Apparently, a plane had just crashed near the airport, and the only information provided in the radio broadcast was that the plane had departed from Chicago. It turned out to be the US Air flight that I chose not to take, for reasons that were largely happenstance. There had been 132 passengers on board, and there were no survivors.

It would be nice if I could say that singular event changed something in me. Made me more spiritual, made me more grateful, made me more aware of the fragility of life. But it mostly conveyed the randomness of events and the possibility that we have little control over certain things. We can't live our lives wondering if each decision we make could be a fatal one. That would be immobilizing. But then came the year 2012, and I was diagnosed with stage 4 lung cancer. That was different. That changed everything.

My knowledge of cancer was limited. I was aware my aunt Ruth had survived multiple cancers, including a mass on her lung that was not identified until she was in her late-70s. She was able to have it surgically removed, and she ultimately lived into her 90s. My grandfather had been diagnosed with lymphoma in his 60s, and had been one of the first cancer patients successfully treated with radiation; his case had been written up in medical journals. My grandmother had been diagnosed with lung cancer in her 80s, but at that point, her doctor chose not to treat it with chemotherapy, as there was a legitimate concern she could not tolerate the side effects. Sometimes the treatment can be worse than the disease. But it had never occurred to me that lung cancer could be genetic, a biological inheritance no one wants to receive.

I thought about this as we navigated through Flagstaff, and toward the South Rim of the Grand Canyon. We spent a few days hiking, and then drove across the state to Las Vegas. Long drives allow you to think and reflect. Arizona is a beautiful state; the blue sky and the desert landscape allowed my mind to wander. I had never thought about my mortality before. I had no reason to. I tried to think about what was in front of me, and I imagined a world where I would be absent. I tried to get my head around my diagnosis, but with Matthew in the back seat, Andrea and I could not discuss this. It was hard.

We arrived in Las Vegas and checked into Treasure Island. It was spring break, and the hotel was packed. The casino reeked of smoke, and for a newly diagnosed lung cancer patient, it was, to say the least, off-putting. Andrea walked through the casino with a handkerchief over her face, and then she and Matthew went to wait outside. I figured that since I had already been diagnosed with lung cancer, a little smoke wasn't going to hurt me.

I stood in the check-in line for 45 minutes, listened to the ceaseless bing-bing-bing sound of the slot machines, and was surprised at my newfound patience. When you are told you have a terminal disease, you really do stop sweating the small stuff. We checked in, grabbed a quick dinner, and then went off to see a Cirque du Soleil production at The Mirage, the one set to songs from the Beatles.

There is something very inspiring about music. It can transport you away from your day-to-day troubles and let you imagine another world. It can touch you in a place that is hard to get to. It reaches into the soul. Hearing it while seeing the acrobats bouncing high on trampolines, doing aerial tricks, and contorting themselves into extraordinary positions made me wonder if the impossible was indeed possible.

The performers flew above the stage in ways that defied gravity. When "Get Back" played, I listened to the lyrics, and the line about getting "back to where you once belonged" resonated deeply. How could I get back to a world I inhabited a mere two weeks ago, a world where I could plan on a long, happy life, where my mortality would not be staring me in the face? I thought about the 5-year life expectancy for people like me, and even though the data only gave me a 10 percent chance, I wondered what that 10 percent did to survive. How could I beat the odds? How could I become one of *those guys*?

I began to feel something stir inside of me. I had quickly grown weary of thinking about my mortality. I did not want to feel terrified. I started thinking about possibilities. I began to have some optimism, even though I had no logical reason to do so. And while I still knew very little about my disease or the actual prognoses, I did know that miracles happen. They happen every day. And I began to believe that I could be one of them.

We drove home the next day. It was a Sunday, and the drive was remarkably pleasant. And so on a warm Monday afternoon, I went to The Angeles Clinic in Santa Monica to meet Dr. Daniel Lieber and begin the next phase of my life.

4

Picking An Oncologist

I have made a career out of asking people questions. Marketing research is a field in which we design surveys and moderate focus groups and conduct in-depth interviews. The goal is for companies to better understand their customers' opinions, and it's used to guide decision-making in business. I am naturally curious, so coming up with questions is easy for me. Writing questionnaires and discussion guides was my favorite part of work, and I had spent almost 30 years at it, the last 12 at DirecTV. I liked the challenge of crafting questions that would allow us to understand consumer opinions and even evoke a depth of feeling. The way in which the questions are worded, the scale of answers to choose from, and even the order of the questions can impact the results of the research. When executed properly, people feel surprisingly comfortable about sharing some of their innermost feelings.

When Andrea and I met with Dr. Lieber, I naturally peppered him with dozens of questions, some good, some awful, and some simply unanswerable. To Dr. Lieber's credit, he addressed every question I had calmly and thoroughly and honestly. I asked the practical questions about which treatments were available to me and what were the likely outcomes – including possible side effects. I asked if herbal remedies were effective. I asked whether a positive attitude could cure cancer. I asked whether the cancer might just go away on its own. I asked so many questions that I now cringe thinking back on this. But one thing I distinctly recall is that Dr. Lieber never rolled his eyes, never looked impatient, and always had an intelligent response, even to the most absurd question.

In retrospect, this was unusual; future appointments with other doctors did not go this swimmingly. Dr. Lieber said he wanted me to be comfortable with whatever treatment plan we mutually decided on, and for me, this was preeminent. Doctors do the best they can, but in the end, it is the patient, not the doctor, who has to live or die with the outcomes. And if I had to accept the outcomes, I absolutely wanted a say in what we did.

I had been diagnosed with adenocarcinoma, a form of non-small cell lung cancer, the most common type of lung cancer there was, particularly among non-smokers. What I learned from Dr. Lieber that day was that significant advancements were indeed being made in treating this disease. Whereas chemotherapy, a shotgun blast of toxins into the body, had been the standard treatment for years, targeted therapy was a newer approach that worked to stop the growth of specific cancer cells. It is sometimes referred to as precision, or personalized, medicine. For me, this would involve little more than taking a few pills each day, and what Dr. Lieber told me next made a lot of sense.

"If you have a choice, it's better to take a pill than to take chemotherapy."

One of the big problems with chemotherapy had been it not only killed cancer cells in the body, but it was indiscriminate, meaning it also killed healthy cells. It was also hard to tolerate; it could lead to hair loss, massive fatigue, and severe digestive issues. My internet research told me that chemo was considered the drug of last resort. Targeted therapy was a more precise way of identifying and attacking cancerous tumors, so they could no longer grow and could no longer spread to critical parts of the body.

There were some harsh realities to be faced, however. Doctors had to be able to identify the exact genetic mutation of the tumor, because these targeted therapies could only be effective on specific types of tumors. Dr. Lieber recommended doing a biopsy of the tumor as soon as possible, to see what my options were. But the reality was that only about one-half of tumors could be identified at that point, and many new treatments were still in development.

I also asked some tough questions. My parents had both lived long lives. What were the chances I would reach my 80s? He answered honestly, that given my diagnosis, the chances were not good, but he also added that it was not impossible, either. He told me every oncologist has patients who survive cancer and live for a long time. Doctors do not always know why this happens, why some patients respond well to treatment and others do not. He told me had been treating a few stage 4 cancer patients for more than 15 years. My eyes grew wide. That was what I wanted to hear. That meant hope.

With regard to alternative treatments, Dr. Lieber was skeptical. He was, after all, a scientist, and he believed in traditional medicine because he knew it had a better chance of working. He did not discount herbal remedies, but he also did not believe them to be nearly as effective. When I asked him whether a positive attitude could have an impact, he said it absolutely could, but more in the area of maintaining a good quality of life. The medicine, he believed, would be the ultimate arbiter of my longevity.

Still, there was a school of thought that said a positive outlook could possibly make a patient's body more open to the medicine. Andrea had done her doctoral dissertation on the impact of the unconscious on fertility, and found numerous cases of couples unable to conceive after years of trying – and yet soon after adopting a child, some of these women became pregnant. There was a lot we were still learning about how the mind affected the body.

Shortly after we met with Dr. Lieber, I read an article about Steve Jobs, who had been diagnosed with pancreatic cancer a few years earlier. He believed that adopting a diet consisting mainly of fruit was the best response to his illness, and this protocol could send him into remission. Sadly, that was far from the case, and he acknowledged this before his death. He said he wished he had listened to his doctors and stuck to Western medicine.

There are four stages to lung cancer. Each stage describes how far the disease has spread. Stage 1 is considered early stage, where one tumor is found, isolated in only one lung, and it can be successfully removed through surgery. Stage 2 is where multiple tumors are found in the lung, but again, they have not spread to another part of the body. Stage 3 is where the cancer has spread from the lung to other nearby tissue, sometimes to the lymph nodes, sometimes to the pleural or chest area, next to the lung.

At stage 3, surgery is not practical because the cancer is located in more than one area. And then there is stage 4, which means the cancer has spread from the lung to other organs, or to the bones or the brain. In my case, the scans showed that the cancer had spread to the liver, kidney, and lymph nodes. This is sometimes called advanced lung cancer, which is a polite way of saying this is the end stage, the one before you die. Thankfully, Dr. Lieber never called it anything remotely like that.

I am very lucky in a number of regards, one of which is access to great doctors. But I also had the remarkably good fortune to have not one, but two family members, cousins, who were oncologists. They both spent a lot of time answering questions and providing ideas. My cousin Paul Baron sought out the top oncologists in California and referred me to Dr. Ronald Natale, a lung cancer specialist at Cedars-Sinai Medical Center, who was considered one of the leading experts in the field. I met with him shortly after meeting with Dr. Lieber, and he was clearly a brilliant doctor. Dr. Natale explained how the various treatments worked, as well as what to expect. He was keenly aware of the most current data, and he laid out the options available to me. He explained the genetic mutations they were aware of and the treatments that were being used to address them. He spoke calmly and intelligently, detailing what the life expectancy would be for each treatment, citing these in terms of months. As the reality sank in, I began to get a very queasy feeling. My mouth tightened and I felt my breath coming in spurts. I did my best to focus on something positive, but I had an uneasy sense that my optimism was beginning to slip away.

Dr. Natale agreed a biopsy was necessary, but he had some reservations about the pleurodesis. He told me there was a possibility that this procedure could trap cancer cells in a place where the chemo would be unable to reach them. He acknowledged his theory was not proven, it was simply a concern of his. But as we talked, Dr. Natale stopped all of a sudden and seemed to process everything. He then said that in considering my situation, a pleurodesis made the most sense for someone like me, largely because it could help prevent a collapsed lung, which was a more imminent threat. This was obviously a more pressing concern than having cancer cells trapped in a place where the chemo could not destroy them. His advice made sense.

Afterward, Andrea and I walked across the street to a deli for lunch. She asked me how I felt about this doctor. Between bites of a corned beef sandwich, I said that as brilliant as Dr. Natale was, I sensed he was more of a scientist. I also came away from the meeting feeling very gloomy about my prognosis. The data he presented was strikingly depressing, and the treatment options were explained in stark, clinical detail. He was very frank and honest, and he laid out my prospects in sharp detail. He was very fair. He told me of the probable life expectancy that various types of treatments held, and he did so in terms I could grasp, which is to say, in terms I found mortifying. It made me think back to what Dr. Wellington, the respiratory specialist, had alluded to a few weeks back, when I first learned about my diagnosis.

"I know a number of patients who have been living with lung cancer for three years now."

Different doctors are right for different patients. I needed one who was willing to partner with me on this journey. I was sure Dr. Natale was very smart and would answer all my questions, but I was less certain he would be a good partner. In choosing a leading expert as my primary oncologist, I would likely feel pressured to follow his recommendations.

In my experience, experts don't always like to be challenged with alternate ideas, especially from a layman like myself. It also occurred to me that if I were to ask about consulting with another lung cancer specialist, or tell him I wanted a second opinion, this might seem insulting. I didn't know this for certain, it was just a feeling I got. He was brutally honest, which is not unreasonable, although having your longevity laid out so starkly drove home a point I didn't want to consider. He never actually said it, but it didn't take much for me to put the pieces together and formulate a conclusion. There was a good likelihood I would die soon.

Dr. Lieber was a generalist, but he told me he regularly huddled with specialists, and when there were any conflicting opinions, he would simply talk to more specialists. So, to me, it made sense to see an oncologist who had a large network of experts to consult. With the number of questions I was bound to ask, I needed someone with whom I could have an open dialogue. Dr. Lieber fielded all of my questions easily, and I felt like I was having a comfortable conversation. I walked out of his office feeling optimistic about things. In contrast, after my meeting with Dr. Natale, my feeling was that I'd like to find the nearest tall building, go up to the roof, and jump off. I thought back to what Dr. Lieber had told me about maintaining a positive attitude. It wouldn't impact my longevity, but it was important for having a better quality of life.

And at that moment, everything crystallized. I decided to have Dr. Lieber be my primary oncologist. One issue resolved, but there would be many more to come.

5

Picking A Surgeon

The first thing Dr. Lieber recommended we do was address the fluid in my lung. In addition to having a pleurodesis to fix this issue, we needed to biopsy the lung tumor, and both of these things could be done in one procedure. He referred me to two different thoracic surgeons, and I again began to see the vital importance of selecting the right doctor.

Both doctors were associated with thoracic surgery units in large hospitals in Los Angeles. But when I spoke with the first one, who I'll call Dr. Bumstead, he actively tried to sell me on having the pleurodesis with him, an interaction which made me recoil. He told me that the pleurodesis could cure cancer, something that sounded quite odd. I asked Dr. Lieber about how accurate this was, and he immediately debunked this notion. When I tried to get Dr. Bumstead back on the phone to clarify, he never returned my calls. And when I went online to take a look at his background, there was very little about him on the internet. It was almost as if someone had gone in and wiped away any information about Dr. Bumstead, which made me even more leery.

One thing I've learned about making decisions in the business world is, all things being equal, to trust my gut. If something feels wrong about a situation, there usually is something wrong. Intuition is defined as being able to understand a situation without conscious reasoning. It's sometimes referred to as a sixth sense. On a more practical note, when someone you have just met tells you an untruth, it is a pretty good bet they will continue to tell you more untruths. Interestingly, Dr. Bumstead would soon leave his position at the hospital, for reasons no one seemed willing to discuss. In a bizarre twist, I would encounter Dr. Bumstead again a few years later, and my concerns here would later be validated.

I then spoke to the other surgeon, Dr. Robert McKenna, who was more informative and more knowledgeable than Dr. Bumstead, and he did not try and sell me on the procedure. He also dismissed the notion that this procedure could provide a cure for cancer. He told me the pleurodesis was simply a preventive measure that was very effective at stopping the fluid buildup in the lung, not a cure for cancer. When I asked how complicated a pleurodesis would be, he answered that for a surgeon like him, it was as routine a procedure as it got. He had done lots of them. For me, that was what I needed to hear. I like an experienced hand. We scheduled the procedure for the following week. There was no reason to wait.

In my 55 years, I had never spent a night in a hospital. I had never been to an ER or to Urgent Care.

I had been fortunate to have had good health up to this point, and the added benefit was that I had no idea of what to expect. As such, I did not have a lot of worries or apprehensions about having an invasive procedure, or about staying in a hospital for a couple of nights. It is the blessing of an uncluttered mind. Even ignorance has an upside.

The procedure took about 45 minutes. The anesthesiologist told me I'd be asleep after he'd counted backward from 10. I recall him counting down to 9 and then 8, and then the next thing I knew I was being wheeled out of the operating room, the procedure completed. I spent the rest of the next two days doing little more than watching ESPN in my room, with Andrea bringing food over from local restaurants. We still hadn't told Matthew yet, a conversation I could not keep putting off. We simply told him I was going in for some tests.

Dr. McKenna also performed a biopsy in order to do genetic mapping of the tumor. This would determine if I could potentially take a targeted therapy, a pill, rather than go through chemo. I rested for the remainder of the day, and since they had me on painkillers, it was not an altogether unpleasant experience, and I slept well that night. Most of the nurses were men, and we got along fine. On the last day, however, a new nurse on duty was insistent about reinstalling a catheter that had been giving me some discomfort the day before. I asked the nurse to get a doctor's opinion, and he said that wasn't necessary.

When a nurse tells you a doctor's opinion isn't necessary, it is a good time to demand another nurse.

After a good bit of arguing, I finally yelled at him that there was a better chance of me tossing him headfirst out the window than there was of him reinstalling the catheter. The head of the unit had to come in and intercede, and he finally transferred the nurse to a different part of the floor. When the doctor on duty finally arrived, he agreed that reinstalling the catheter wasn't necessary.

This unexpected confrontation reinforced my sense that I had to be the one making the final decisions about my body, albeit in consultation with people who knew what they were talking about. I needed to become my own best advocate, and not blindly trust what one person told me. From doctors on down, no one had perfect information; it would be up to me to sort through the options and then make the final call.

The pleurodesis turned out to be very effective; I no longer had any pain in my back. But the results of the biopsy did not show any identifiable genetic mutations in my lung tumor. So, in addition to surgery no longer being an option, neither was a targeted therapy. I would not be able to just take a pill. The one treatment still available to me was the one I most dreaded.

Chemotherapy, the drug of last resort, was now the one staring me in the face. It was the final option.

6

The Toughest Conversation

The decisions a cancer patient faces are unending. While my treatment options were now limited to chemotherapy, there were numerous types of chemo to choose from. The first was Alimta, a relatively new drug that was developed for patients with lung cancer, and considered milder than other chemo options. Dr. Lieber consulted with another lung cancer specialist who thought I should use Taxol, a more traditional chemo. Taxol was known to be very potent, but the side effects were harsher. That specialist reviewed my file and noticed my T cell count was high. He had a theory that patients with high T cells did not respond as well to Alimta. T cells are part of the immune system and can work to attack cancer cells when detected within the body.

I asked Dr. Lieber if he could consult with a few other lung cancer specialists to see if there was any consensus on this. I also asked Cousin Paul, and he spoke with a lung cancer specialist he knew. All came back with the same response. It was possible Alimta might not work well on me, but it was also possible it could. The doctor's T cell theory was just that – a theory. Possible, but unproven as yet. And I didn't feel like being a lab rat, where following this doctor's suggestion would simply add to his data, while I'd be living with the nasty side effects.

By this point, I had started reading some books on how other patients dealt with the trauma of being diagnosed with cancer, as well as how to deal with extraordinary situations. I tried reading *When Bad Things Happen To Good People* but found it to be distasteful. The author was a rabbi who believed prayer was useless, and that the world was controlled solely by human beings. He seemed to believe God was doing little more than hovering in the background as a bystander. I had never been an exceptionally religious person, but I was not about to discount the power of prayer.

I bought a copy of Hamilton Jordan's book, *No Such Thing As A Bad Day*, which chronicled his 20-plus years of experience dealing with various cancers. He advocated that patients needed to be in charge of making the decisions for their own bodies, taking into account doctors' advice, but recognizing that doctors are not always correct in their decisions. This was totally in line with what I had been experiencing, and I was thrilled to see someone else articulate it so well. I began to formulate a game plan of my own.

Aided by this way of thinking, I started doing my own research, still using the internet, trying to separate the nuggets from the turds. My goal was not to get advice, but rather to learn the effects that Alimta and Taxol had had on other patients. Understanding the experiences of others is profoundly valuable. Hearing about what other patients had gone through was a window into what I could expect to go through.

I learned that Taxol was indeed very harsh and much more likely to lead to neuropathy, which is intense pain in the fingers and toes. It was also more likely to cause hair loss, severe stomach aches, and just about every bad thing one could imagine when pumping something akin to poison into the human body. For some people, Taxol held their best chance of survival, so I understood the rationale. But I also got the feeling that if another option was possible, I should consider it. Some people call this taking the easy way out; I called it living your best life under the worst circumstances.

Patients on Alimta did not have as severe a reaction as those on Taxol, although it varied with the person. Another discovery, and quite an important one: different people react differently to the same treatment. Some patients may have acute problems, some will handle it fine. My other oncologist cousin, Steve Neudorf, told me that doctors aren't really sure why certain people thrive for many years on a given treatment, while others do not. There were a lot of unknowns out there. Medicine was still an art as much as it was a science.

I went back to Dr. Lieber and asked if I could start with Alimta. If it didn't work we could always transition to Taxol, but I thought it would be best to begin with the easiest treatment and see if it was effective. There was also no guarantee that Taxol, the harsher chemo, would be any more effective for me. He agreed, and told me we could always move on to something else if Alimta didn't work. We were walking through the fog of uncertainty, but I felt as if we were headed in the right direction. Before I moved forward though, I needed to start telling people about my cancer. And most of all, I needed to tell one person in particular. I needed to tell my son.

When my diagnosis was confirmed during our trip to Arizona, I was only able to talk briefly about it with Andrea. I asked her not to discuss it with anyone at the time, because I felt I needed to get my arms around the whole idea of having a terminal disease, and to understand it better. I had long been a private person, and I had always been guarded about telling people my business. I did not want pity, nor was I ready to deal with discussing my life-threatening condition with others, especially having just learned of it myself. I was not ready to talk about it, and didn't want her to, either.

Looking back, it was unfair of me to ask Andrea to keep quiet about this. She needed someone to talk to. She was a psychologist, and her whole career was about talking with people. But I wanted to shield Matthew from this news until I could prepare myself to have that difficult discussion. I did not want him to find out by overhearing a conversation, or by someone inadvertently mentioning it in front of him. These things happen. I didn't want it to happen to him.

When we had stopped for lunch after leaving the Grand Canyon, Andrea slipped away for a minute and called her brother, Ben, to let him know what was happening. She needed to tell someone. It was too hard to stay quiet about a subject she desperately wanted to discuss. I understand that now. I did not understand it then.

I finally came to a place where I was ready to talk about this with Matthew. I would then begin the process of telling friends and family and colleagues. It was a Saturday afternoon, he had finished his homework and had begun watching a basketball game on TV. Andrea and I asked him to come into the living room to talk. He gave us a strange look. He knew something was up. We did not do this often.

With my hands shaking, I began by telling him about how this all started, the pain in my back, visiting the doctor, and undergoing a battery of tests to find out what was wrong. I told him that I had been diagnosed with lung cancer, but I tried to reassure him that there were bold new treatments available, some amazing advances being made, and scientists were on their way to finding a cure. I tried to present this as little more than a minor obstacle for us, an inconvenience that we would get through. I tried to sound confident and optimistic. He listened quietly and then asked me, in a somber tone, a question I did not prepare myself for.

"Are you going to die?" he asked.

I paused. There are many dark moments that cancer patients must face. The moment we receive our diagnosis. The moment when we begin treatment. The moment when we wonder if we'll make it. But for me, this was the darkest moment of them all. There was no script for me to read, no road map for me to follow. I was making this up as I went, doing what parents should not do in these instances, trying to shield our son from pain. He deserved honesty, but I didn't know if I had it in me to be as honest as I needed to be. I was giving him bravado. I had to do better. But I also didn't have much of a plan.

"No," I told him, taking a deep breath and literally crossing my fingers. "I plan to live for a long time. There are a lot of options out there. This is just a bump in the road. It's going to be okay."

At that point, Matthew turned to Andrea and demanded to know what was really going on. "Dad's trying to sugarcoat this, isn't he?!"

Andrea tried her best to reassure Matthew, but he saw right through that, too. We had wanted to exude confidence, even though our confidence had been shaken; it was obvious he wasn't buying it. That our 13-year-old son could see through my bluster with alarming accuracy was unnerving. And at that point, I decided to simply tell him what I knew. He had a right to know the truth, and a right to grieve. It was unfair of me to deny him that.

Thus began a painful discussion. I found it terribly upsetting for him to recognize there was indeed a chance I might die soon. I didn't want him to see me as weak. I didn't want him to see me as sickly. I had always tried to be present in ways he could admire. My own father was never the kind of role model I wanted to emulate, so I had always tried to be different from him. I knew, from my own harsh experience, that children who have an unsatisfactory role model can have great difficulty adjusting to adulthood. It is a very tricky balancing act to present my own frailties, and still be a father my son could look up to.

I told Matthew we really didn't know what the future held, just that there were lots of treatments being developed. I told him things were uncertain. We didn't know what my outcome would be, and that would be a challenge for all of us. But I did also say there were doctors working toward turning cancer into a chronic condition, treatable and manageable. And there really were people living long lives with cancer. I just needed to find the path that was right for me. It was going to be hard at times, and it was going to be scary. There was a reason to worry, but there was also a reason for optimism. Some people survived just fine, and there was no reason to believe I couldn't be one of those people. I tried to provide him with hope. I tried to provide myself with hope. Sometimes that's the only thing we have.

7

Battling Through Depression

It is not uncommon for newly diagnosed cancer patients to experience depression. The future becomes daunting. We don't know how long we'll be able to live with this disease. We don't know how our families will get by financially without us. Anxiety and worry can become part of our everyday fabric. Life as we know it is altered.

I had experienced a bout of depression once before, and it was awful, to say the least. Four years earlier, in 2008, Andrea and I decided we could afford to buy a new house. We had moved into our tiny 2-bedroom cottage in West L.A. a decade earlier. Over time, the value of that house increased, I had earned some nice bonuses at work, and I had even received some stock in DirecTV. Andrea's parents had recently passed away, and left her some money. The economy was doing well, my job was secure, and we had largely outgrown our starter home. We could afford something better.

We started the process by making an offer on a home about a mile away from where we lived. It was about twice the square footage of the home we were in. We made the offer on a lazy Tuesday afternoon in early September. The date was September 9, 2008. A few months earlier, we had lost out in a bidding war for a house in the same neighborhood, and so we became determined that we were going to get this one. It would be ours. We would not be denied this time.

The process started with what's called a real estate agent caravan, held on a Tuesday, four or five days before the standard Sunday open house. The open house is where legitimate buyers, as well as curious neighbors, converge to walk through the home and view the interior. Our realtor had alerted us that this house was about to come on the market soon, and she suggested we take an early look at it during the Tuesday caravan. By a not-so-funny coincidence, the listing agent happened to be our realtor's brother.

It was a nice home. The layout was remarkably similar to the house we lost out on, and the list price was nearly identical, too. It was much bigger than our current home, and the neighborhood was better as well. Even the lawn looked to be a deeper shade of green. It wasn't exactly our dream home; it was 60 years old and would need some updating. But after years of trudging through a myriad of open houses, this felt good, and good seemed good enough. I did the math and decided we could almost afford it. A few cutbacks here, a little belt-tightening there, and we'd be fine. All seemed right.

That night we made a full-price offer on the house with only the standard contingencies – loan approval and inspection. The sellers clarified some terms, and a few days later we both signed. Andrea and I had bought ourselves a new home, and we did it before the sellers had even conducted their first Sunday open house. We were in. Grabbed it before anyone else had even looked at it. We patted ourselves on the back for having the guile to pull the trigger before anyone else could even draw. So, armed with an optimism that seems almost unique to the uninformed, we began our march into an unseemly hell, one that would take years for us to get our investment back.

We quickly readied our current house for sale, which only took a week or two. At the beginning of that year, we had re-painted, re-carpeted, and de-cluttered our house in anticipation of this moment. Our realtor complimented us on what a wonderful job we did in getting our home ready to show. She used words like charming and cute to describe our now comparatively small abode. We set what we thought to be a reasonable list price, and then we waited for the multiple offers to roll in. I even began considering a strategy for the selection process.

This was in mid-September 2008. What was about to happen next was something few people expected. Lehman Brothers, a pillar of Wall Street, announced it was on the verge of bankruptcy. The stock market plummeted, and before we knew it, the bottom had dropped out of the global financial sector.

The treasury secretary began spreading the word of an impending worldwide financial catastrophe. The entire country of Iceland was now dead broke. Major financial institutions were disappearing, and worldwide panic had begun to set in. Not surprisingly, real estate values on the westside of Los Angeles collapsed, too. At the precise moment we needed stability, the world became astonishingly unstable.

And yet the purchase process of our new home roared ahead unabated. The sellers had given us just two weeks to get loan approval, and we did it. Our financial documents were in order, the bank moved forward quickly on approving our mortgage, and the home inspection looked good. So, by the end of September, we were well on our way toward owning a new home, even as I wondered if there would be problems selling the old one. Something felt very wrong.

At the end of September, we held our first open house, and our realtor told us afterward that we had a lot of "traffic." Despite the cratering economy, she told us a number of people were openly discussing what offer to make. We began to feel better about the possibility of a quick sale and sat back to await the offers.

Only it didn't quite happen that way. The next day, Monday, we awoke to the news of further financial meltdowns on Wall Street. As the day progressed, the Dow Jones index plunged nearly 800 points, which, at that time, made it one of the biggest single-day declines in history. The TV talking heads were openly warning of a looming economic depression, similar to the one seen in the 1930s. They were anticipating many people would lose their jobs, not get new ones, and experience financial ruin. Needless to say, the multiple offers we anticipated never materialized.

September came and went, and the Dow Jones continued its freefall, nose-diving from over 11,000 in mid-September to 8,000 in mid-October. The upshot of this impacted the real estate market in two pivotal ways. Potential buyers now had a lot less money to use toward a down payment, which also meant there were suddenly fewer serious buyers. Buyers who had stuffed their money in a mattress rather than in stocks were still looking at houses. But they were more discriminating, and far less inclined to pay anywhere near list price. They were seeking bargains. In addition, rumors were agog that banks were now becoming much more strict in their lending practices, which is to say they would no longer give mortgages to anybody who simply asked for one.

In business, one is often subjected to the whim of fate. You don't want to be in the market to buy a house when prices are escalating rapidly, because you can get into a bidding war and pay too much. Conversely, you don't want to be selling a house when the market is cold, because the buyers can dictate price. For those buying a new house while selling their old house, this usually becomes a moot point, because you typically benefit in either the purchase or the sale. But Andrea and I had just purchased our new home in a seller's market, and within only a few weeks, we were trying to sell our current home in a buyer's market. There is actually a military term that captures this type of unusual predicament. It is called a clusterfuck.

But life goes on. Our realtor continued to have open houses on our old home, even though traffic was much slower and buyers were becoming even more fickle. Many were asking how low we would go on price. No one wanted to buy our house for anywhere near what we were asking.

The escrow process on our new home was moving along just fine. The media was reporting on how tough it was for buyers to get a mortgage. Not for us, though. Our loan process was remarkably easy, and we were about to be the proud owners of two homes, both plummeting in value. The money I had invested in my retirement plan was tied to the stock market, meaning its value had also dropped like a rock.

As the extent of the global financial crisis began to unfold, a change came over me. My sleep pattern had gone from 8 hours a night to 5 hours to 3 hours. I lost 5 pounds, which, on the surface, might have been a good thing; I could have stood to drop a few pounds. The problem was I had not been trying to lose any weight. I was not eating any differently. Something else was going on.

One night I found myself watching USC's football team losing to Oregon State, and I felt absolutely nothing. Having earned a Master's degree at USC, and being a big fan of the Trojans, I normally get very animated when I watch them play. I become physically agitated when the team is losing. I often feel the need to help the team along by providing loud and obnoxious coaching tips, even when the game is being played a few miles – or a few thousand miles – away. That night, Matthew expressed surprise at why I wasn't yelling at the TV. I was wondering the same thing. I could see the game in front of me, but I couldn't *feel* the game. In a normal world, this might be perceived as a positive step forward toward maturity and growth. But in this case, I simply felt numb. It was as if I were falling into a state that bordered on clinical depression.

I read and re-read the contract we signed for the new house, and it had no loopholes. I wondered if it was worth backing out of the deal, even if it meant losing our deposit. I showed the contract to a real estate attorney, and he pointed out we could lose a lot more than just our deposit. Since the value of our new home had obviously dropped significantly in the past month, the seller could sue us to make up for any losses he incurred if we chose to not go through with the sale. This could mean we'd be on the hook for hundreds of thousands of dollars, as the real estate market had suddenly plunged. The attorney tried to calm us by saying he had been in a somewhat similar situation almost 20 years earlier; he had bought a new house and then couldn't sell his old one for nearly a year. In the end, it worked out okay for him, but it did not make me feel assured. I felt myself physically shaking.

There are times when we come up against things that are unpleasant. No one escapes these times. It is the ebb and flow of existence. It can affect us through unemployment, devastating illness, breakup of a relationship, death of a loved one.

There we were, seeing a boatload of money we had earned and saved over the years disappear in a matter of weeks. If there was any solace to be taken, it was in the fact that an awful lot of other people were suffering, too – and in some cases, much worse than us. I still had a job. But it did not make me feel any better knowing others had bigger hardships than we did. Misery may love company, but it is still misery. Our problems would not be going away anytime soon.

Needless to say, I had been doing various calculations on how we might afford to carry two mortgages and two lines of credit. The lines of credit we had established at that point were invoked simply to bridge what might have been a few weeks difference between the purchase of our new home and the sale of our old home. But this temporary situation was now looking more and more permanent. To make myself feel even worse, I created a number of spreadsheets to examine our financial situation under various scenarios, each being worse than the one before. At least I'd know what to expect when hell froze over.

The reality was, if we didn't sell or rent our old house soon, we'd be losing a lot of money. That was assuming I kept my job, of course, and with announcements like Citibank laying off 50,000 employees, my stomach began forming some large knots. The 3 hours a night of sleep I was getting became a regular thing. And my 5-pound weight loss turned into 10 pounds. One friend tried to cheer us up by saying how cool it was that we would own two pieces of real estate on the tony westside of Los Angeles. It did not feel cool. It did not feel good.

One day, some good news seemed to materialize, at least for a moment. Our realtor told us a buyer had suddenly made us an offer on our old house. The only problem was their price was far below what we were asking. What they had presented was something that is called a lowball offer.

My first reaction was to tell them to forget it. After a bit of reflection, however, an offer – even a bad offer – was not to be trifled with in this market. So, we figured we'd make a counteroffer that met them halfway. Good bargaining strategy. A reasonable parry to their opening move. See what they come back with. We passed them our counteroffer. And then we waited. And waited. And waited some more. The sounds of silence rang. The buyers had changed their minds.

We closed escrow on our new home in mid-November. Our new home purchase was now official. That night, I had a horrible nightmare, and the final scene in it depicted a big yellow sign, which said "Game Over." From that point on, 5 hours of sleep sounded like bliss, but it also sounded unattainable. I had never experienced depression, I didn't know much about it at all, yet here I was sliding right into it.

My weight loss was now clocking in at 15 pounds. For the first time in my life, I was actively trying to put weight on. From foot-long sandwiches at Subway (don't forget the extra mayo!) to loaves of sourdough bread slathered with butter. Ice cream sundaes. Real Pepsi, not diet. Bacon cheeseburgers. I could eat anything I wanted with no concern about becoming heavy, which should have been a superpower, but that was hardly the case. The added calories did stem the weight loss, but I wasn't gaining any of the lost weight back. It was very obvious just how much stress was now churning through my body.

November turned into December. The air was cold and motionless. John Lennon once wrote that nobody told him there would be days like these, but he didn't say anything about weeks or months. Every Sunday morning we'd spiff our old home up nicely and then disappear for three hours while our realtor held open houses. Then we'd come back to find no one was interested in making an offer. I was clearly not dealing with this very well.

Andrea's career as a psychologist in private practice afforded her with knowing a lot of people in the field. She mentioned how I was handling this stressful situation to a friend who was a psychiatrist. After I met with him, he prescribed a strong sleeping aid, the thought being that getting sufficient rest was the first step toward dealing with this issue. I took two weeks' vacation over Christmas, got a lot of sleep, and finally I could re-focus my thoughts. We spent the holidays packing and adding a few touches to the new house. We put in some nice floor tile, installed some ceiling lamps, and fixed up a few other things. We tried to make it feel like a home, rather than a money-sucking flesh-eater. We bought Matthew the basketball hoop he had been asking about for years. My mother said she would help us out a little if needed. I finally began to feel a little better. The weight loss reversed itself, and I actually put on a couple of pounds.

I have always found it fascinating how some people can practically have the world fall on them and shrug it off, yet others get irritated at the slightest mishap. How we perceive situations is critical to how we react to them. And I discovered we can often consciously choose what we allow to bother us. And I started to choose not to be bothered by impending financial ruin.

We moved into our new house on December 31, 2008. The move was uneventful, which is to say it went well. The next day was New Year's Day, and Matthew and I watched USC beat Penn State in the Rose Bowl. A new year, new beginnings, things were bound to get better. Our realtor wanted to have more open houses at the start of the year, but we decided to first fix the old house up a little more. We put some staged furniture in and made some cosmetic upgrades and repairs. A few buyers asked to see the house, and we told them no. Not yet. It felt good to be in control of something for a change.

The old house went back on the market in late January. Not holding open houses for 6 weeks, and refusing to show the place, ostensibly had the effect of driving up interest. Potential buyers could only see it from the outside, and with a nice front yard, the property did have good curb appeal. But our long journey into real estate hell continued unabated. We still had buyers sniffing around, but no one was putting in an offer. Then, in late March, our realtor called us, and she gave us some remarkably good news. We had not one, but two offers. Both of them had amazingly come in on the same day.

Interestingly, the two offers were $30,000 apart in price. After studying both, we first chose to negotiate with the lower-priced one, because it was a couple rather than a single person, and they were in better financial straits. We asked them to match what the other buyer had offered. They did. And then a funny thing happened. The two buyers began to engage in a small bidding war on our property.

To say we had just entered a parallel universe was an understatement. For almost six months we could barely entice lowballers to grace us with an insulting offer. But now two parties were fervently negotiating, bidding up the price by the hour. The single person, rather than the couple, ultimately provided us with a much better offer, so we accepted that one. When the dust settled, we had a deal that, while nowhere near our original asking price, was also nowhere near the lowball offer we feared we'd need to accept.

From that point on, the rest went smoothly, and we closed escrow a month later. A light-hearted moment occurred when the couple that had made the original lowball offer months earlier, unaware of our pending deal, asked our realtor how low we'd now be willing to go on price. I didn't even bother with a sarcastic retort. It was our turn to respond with silence. Our flirtation with financial ruin had thankfully come to a close. And my depression was magically gone.

In the end, I think I came out of that experience as a better person. I began to feel truly blessed that I had a steady job, a nice wife and son, and finally, just one mortgage to meet every month. Life became good again. And I also discovered something imperative. Worrying about things you can't control is a recipe for disaster. Depression is a very real thing, and it is debilitating. Having gone through this period, I felt prepared for any bad luck that might come my way. Little did I know that in three short years, I would find myself facing a far more serious situation. You can always earn more money. You cannot always get back your health.

8

Spreading The Word

My cancer diagnosis had been confirmed on March 28, 2012. While I felt it was important to be thorough in plotting out my treatment plan, I also knew I couldn't delay treatment for very long. Cancer moves quickly, and lung cancer is a particularly aggressive cancer. But I also had a job to go to each day, and a paycheck to earn. A number of people on my team had noticed my time out of the office, my more somber mood, and they had expressed genuine concern about my well-being. And my division head, Sebastian, had also observed I was taking a lot of time off.

"Is everything okay?" he asked.

I debated whether to tell him and how much to tell him. I finally decided there was no point in trying to hide what might soon become obvious. I would soon begin taking chemo. While hair loss was not listed as a side effect of Alimta, there were plenty of other complications, not the least of which would be the additional time I'd be taking off from work.

As the director of marketing research, my job involved managing a staff of people who were conducting surveys and interviews and doing data analysis. Earlier in my career, I traveled frequently, but now my job was mostly spent in the office. Meetings were a big part of my day. Much of my job was interacting with executives around the company, understanding what type of consumer information they needed, and finding a method to get it to them. Testing out new ad campaigns, projecting the number of customer defections that would follow a price increase, and measuring customer satisfaction were all part of my job. Managing executive expectations was a part of that as well, and I had gotten used to dealing with difficult people. Designing research studies is not life or death, although some in the entertainment industry would have you think otherwise.

My division head was not a difficult individual *per se,* but he was a demanding one. I had worked under him for almost seven years, and we had established decent communication and a level of trust. Unlike relationships with other bosses I had had in my career, we were not close, but we had a professional interaction that was acceptable. So, I finally told Sebastian about my diagnosis, and the fact that I would need to take some time off for treatment, but I assured him it would not impact my work. I told him I was feeling good about my chances, and that I was determined to beat this disease. He gave me the standard corporate response, that my health was the most important thing, and I should take all the time I needed to deal with this. He also complimented me on my positive attitude. Executives like to see optimism.

I began to tell friends and family and colleagues, and their response was universal disbelief. I was 55 and healthy and a non-smoker. How could I possibly get lung cancer? A number of colleagues mentioned that some other employees at our company had contracted some form of cancer in the past few years. A few noted that I often took a walk after lunch, and wondered if our office's proximity to LAX, the Los Angeles International Airport, might have played a role in my developing lung cancer. But mostly they were shocked. It is ironic that a person who is diagnosed with a terrible disease often has to comfort others when they learn about it. But I had been dealing with this trauma for a few months, and had had some time to process this. I did my best to explain the treatment I would be going through and to try and calm everyone's fears. There, there. It will be fine.

But when it came time to tell my then 88-year-old mother about my illness, I could see a wave of fear sweep across her face, and no amount of reassurance was going to placate her. She asked me if I had talked to Cousin Paul about my cancer, and I confirmed to her that I had. But then, something happened. A calm came over her. She nodded and changed the subject. I think that having had to bury one son was so excruciatingly painful for her, that she did not want to think further about the possibility of having to bury another. Sometimes denial can be a good coping mechanism. It was another peek into the possibility that we can make choices to avoid falling into a depression. Pushing awful thoughts from our minds can be beneficial.

Chemotherapy began during the second week of May, on what coincidentally turned out to be Andrea's birthday. We promised to celebrate her day later. Dr. Lieber wanted me to begin taking folic acid and get a vitamin B12 shot to prep for the chemo. He advised me to stop taking any vitamins and supplements, and also to refrain from eating sushi during this period. Raw fish has a higher risk of being tainted with bacteria, and my immune system would already be strained from dealing with the chemo.

Most importantly, though, Dr. Lieber prescribed a steroid called Decadron to take the day before, during, and after the chemo treatment. The primary purpose was to mask some of the nastier effects of the chemo, of which fatigue was one of the biggest. The Decadron turned out to have an effect similar to that of an amphetamine, helping to get me very amped up. I was incredibly productive during the three days I was on it. The night before I began chemo, I was up past midnight, developing spreadsheets for work, and fully engaged in the task. As strange as that might sound, it also took my mind off what I was about to go through the next day.

I started taking chemo infusions as part of a protocol that's sometimes referred to as a triplet: three types of chemotherapy drugs given on the same day. These were Alimta, Carboplatin, and Avastin, which were designed to hit the cancer cells hard. Because these are strong treatments, especially the Carboplatin, most patients only go on the triplet for 4 to 6 infusions. Doctors refer to these as cycles, with each cycle administered every three weeks.

My ability to tolerate these drugs started out all right, with "all right" meaning only the first couple of days following infusion were problematic. I had an upset stomach at first, something I remedied with ginger candy and probiotic yogurt. My appetite changed over time, however, to the point that the mere thought of all but the blandest food evoked waves of nausea. I needed to take a nap every afternoon, and while that started off as an inconvenience, I soon grew to look forward to it. Having my own office with a door that locked, and no glass walls, made it possible to covertly nod off for half an hour at work. While it was no fun to get hooked up to an IV for a couple of hours and have toxins pumped into my body, the side effects started off as quite tolerable.

The Angeles Clinic had a number of private rooms in its infusion center. Being in Santa Monica, with very well-regarded oncologists, the place treated celebrities now and then. I personally never saw any, but I did ask to use one of the private rooms during my infusion cycles. Getting chemo was fairly routine, and largely uneventful. Each session took a couple of hours, as the chemo slowly dripped into my vein. I mostly spent the time reading, listening to music, or daydreaming. Andrea came along, but I suspect she was as bored as I was.

I am not, by nature, an outgoing person. As a child, I was very introverted, and while I've overcome some of my shyness as an adult, it still can be difficult for me to begin a conversation with a total stranger. Even when the person sitting next to me in the infusion room has a similar disease, I still have pause. It was a failure on my part, and I was shunning these patients in the same way that I feared others would shun me; I just wasn't ready to get too close to someone who might be dying. I had, in some ways, never really gotten past what's often identified as the first stage of grief: denial.

There is a widely held view that people who are ill go through five stages of grief. This idea stems from a book called *On Death and Dying,* by Elizabeth Kübler-Ross. She defined the five stages as denial, anger, bargaining, depression, and acceptance. As I look back, though, I struggle with whether I fully went through all of these stages after being diagnosed.

I had no doubt that my initial reaction to getting cancer was denial. But there was minimal anger. Who could I be angry with? I suppose I was a little angry with God for throwing me into this mess, although the bitterness was not about what I'd be going through, it was more about what my family might have to deal with in the aftermath. I did experience a bout of sadness, and sadness is sometimes defined as anger turned within. So, I suppose I did indeed go through this stage.

There was also no bargaining with a higher power, nor any recriminations on "what if" I had done something differently. I did pray, but it was not about promising to be a better person or changing my life in some profound way. I believed I was already a good person who tried to do the right thing. I simply asked God to lead me down a path toward normalcy. I asked him to do so because it would be better for my wife and son. But I didn't offer up anything in return. I admit my knowledge of prayer was limited. I had recalled Jim Morrison's line that you cannot petition the Lord with prayer, but the Doors singer died of a heroin overdose, and I didn't think he was the expert on spirituality.

I could have easily slipped into a depression, but my past experience with our home sale taught me to try and avoid it at all costs. And I don't think I did go into a real depression. Sadness, for sure, but depression involves taking a bleak outlook on things, and I refused to allow that.

All of that leads to acceptance, and I did accept both my illness and the possible consequences, and I accepted these fairly quickly. I knew what I had, and I knew what I had to do to get better. But acceptance of the illness did not mean I was accepting that my life would end soon. If I was struggling with anything, it was how best to define how I would approach the cancer going forward. I needed to have a clear vision of how I would lead my life from now on. I needed a plan.

9

Cruising The Internet

One of the best things about the internet is you can interact with people while remaining anonymous. It is also one of the worst things about the internet. Despite my not being ready to identify or associate with other cancer patients at that time, I did recognize the need to talk to others who were going through the same issues I was going through. As supportive as friends and family were, it was lung cancer patients who shared the same bond of dealing with what lay ahead. Still, being a little uneasy around new people, I did not want to join any local cancer support groups, nor participate in any in-person meetings. And so for me, the internet became a godsend.

I signed on to a number of cancer forums and soon found my way to a number of lung cancer boards such as Inspire and Cancer Grace, where patients would pose questions, express concerns, offer support and discuss potential remedies. It was part emotional connection, and part sharing of practical knowledge. A few days after my first infusion of chemo, I began to get a bad case of the hiccups late at night. While this might sound amusing, trying to go to sleep with intermittent hiccups became very problematic. I tried everything from breathing into a paper bag to biting into a lemon. I tried lowering my head and drinking a glass of water so that I was swallowing upward. Finally, someone suggested swallowing a spoonful of peanut butter and then holding my breath for 10 seconds. As ridiculous as that sounds, it worked. The hiccups went away.

There was a lot of talk on these forums about herbal and alternative remedies, and some people claimed they were having success with everything from cannabis oil to high doses of vitamin C. I needed to remind myself that many of these people were patients, very desperate to cling to anything which might work for them; these were not scientists engaging in an online discussion.

I came upon some interesting information about legitimate treatments using immunotherapy, as well as some valuable tips on clinical trials. If nothing else, there was a thought-provoking trove of information being bandied about. Patients shared tidbits their doctors had told them, and these exchanges made me more keenly aware of options that were out there, as well as potential pitfalls. One person warned us to be wary of clinical trials where one-half the group was given a placebo, or a sugar pill, while the other half got the actual drug.

These online communities provided good support, but with a caveat. Talking with other patients had a lot of value, but it also involved some risk, too. Not everyone knew what they were talking about. One woman who was recently diagnosed with stage 4 lung cancer expressed a lot of fears, and said she was really scared. The group rose up to provide encouragement and tell her everything was going to be okay. A few people even employed the phrase, "You got this!" Her sister came onto the site about a month later to tell us the woman had passed away. Bolstering someone's confidence can be valuable. Giving them false hope without understanding their situation is not.

Some of the comments that patients made about their doctors made me feel very good about having Dr. Lieber as my oncologist. I had been told that, in medicine, the smartest doctors often go into the more challenging fields like oncology and neurology. These fields tend to be more interesting. But even within oncology, some are simply better at understanding their job than others – they work harder, they're more aware of advances in the field, and they are also more sensitive to patients' needs.

One incident with Dr. Lieber really had an impact on me. He told me he was going away for a few days to attend his daughter's graduation from college, and then did something unusual. He not only gave me his personal cell phone number, but he also gave me his wife's cell phone number – just in case I needed to reach him while he was on the phone with someone else. Whenever I had an appointment with Dr. Lieber, he would frequently be interrupted by his staff with incoming phone calls, sometimes from patients, sometimes from insurance companies, sometimes from other doctors. His ability to juggle so many issues effectively, and to move effortlessly from one subject to another was amazing. As I would later learn, however, that type of intense work takes its toll on a person.

As I read about the experiences of patients around the world, it was obvious that some doctors were unaware of the keen advances being made in lung cancer. In a few instances, it felt as if some of these patients knew as much as their oncologists did. These online interactions often made patients more informed. Not every lung cancer patient was being tested for genetic mutations at that time, and this was especially true overseas. Some patients complained they had not been told about other options, and were immediately put on chemo. Others didn't understand why their doctor had chosen a certain type of chemo, and still others were not being directed to take folic acid or Decadron prior to their chemo treatments.

I learned it is never a good idea to simply put your fate in someone else's hands, even a qualified doctor, without at least understanding why certain protocols were being done. Asking questions was part of my nature; finding out why things were the way they were intrigued me. My mother once told me that nearly as soon as I started walking, I began to run into stores and shops whenever we went out – much to her frustration, as she was frequently running after me, trying to forestall whatever havoc I was about to wreak. I was simply curious about things. When I was four years old I remember I went to the dentist, and when he went out of the room I decided to play ship's captain with his X-ray machine. Unfortunately, he wasn't aware of my proclivity to touch and play with everything I could get my hands on. He was not at all happy when I wound up breaking his X-ray machine; my parents were even less happy that they had to foot the bill to pay for the repairs.

Early on in my treatment, I happened to reconnect with an old friend, Jennifer, from my years of working at Disney Channel back in the 1990s. Her boyfriend had ironically also been diagnosed with stage 4 lung cancer, years before. He was a former sergeant in the Marine Corps, which allowed him to be treated at the Veterans Affairs Hospital in Westwood. After a year of chemotherapy, the VA doctors told him the treatments were no longer working, and they advised him to go home and "get his affairs in order," which is code for preparing yourself to die.

Jennifer desperately called her network of friends, pleading for suggestions. One advised that they go see Dr. Robert Nagourney in Long Beach, who often took patients other doctors had given up on. Dr. Nagourney experimented with a drug cocktail that immediately worked for Jennifer's boyfriend. But two years later, the cancer returned. Dr. Nagourney then did a biopsy on the tumor and profiled the tissue, meaning they tested various drugs on the tumor before beginning any treatment. They discovered there was a positive response to the drug Tarceva. The common wisdom was Tarceva only worked on tumors with a very specific genetic mutation called EGFR, and he had tested negative for that mutation. But without other options, Tarceva looked like a possible answer for him, so he began taking it. Incredibly, it was effective, and he was able to stay on that drug for more than a decade.

It struck me there was a lot of information about cancer treatments that doctors didn't fully understand yet. But they were learning. And they were making advances. I didn't know it at the time, but I would soon be one of the beneficiaries of all that progress.

10

The Clinical Trial

Early on, I had asked Dr. Lieber about clinical trials, and he promised he would look into them, although he cautioned me that trials were experiments. Nonetheless, shortly after my first chemo infusion, he informed me about a clinical trial at the University of California Irvine, for a drug called Crizotinib (pronounced Criz-AH-tin-ib). The drug was referred to as a TKI, or a tyrosine kinase inhibitor. That meant it targeted and worked to inhibit proteins that allowed cancer cells to grow, replicate, and move to other parts of the body. The TKI would take control of the cancer's "on-off switch" and effectively block the signals that tell the cancer cells to divide and spread to other parts of the body.

Crizotinib was administered by way of a pill, and had received FDA approval for patients whose lung cancer had a mutation called the ALK gene. When a new cancer drug is effective on one type of mutation, scientists try to find out if it will work on other mutations as well. The Crizotinib trial at UC Irvine was with patients who tested positive for a newly discovered genetic mutation called the ROS1 (pronounced Ross One) Rearrangement. Although this was a somewhat rare mutation, Dr. Lieber felt we had nothing to lose by checking to see if I had this mutation, especially since I just had a biopsy done.

This genetic mutation was called the ROS1 Rearrangement because the ROS1 gene attaches itself to a healthy gene and changes, or rearranges, the composition of the gene. This gene then creates an abnormal protein, which allows it to replicate quickly and enter healthy tissues in other parts of the body. Then it quickly repeats the process. What the Crizotinib drug does is attach itself to the ROS1 cells, inhibiting their ability to multiply. The ROS1 cells then stop behaving like cancer, and this ultimately causes the cells to die off.

We set up an appointment at the UC Irvine Medical Center, which is technically not in Irvine, or anywhere near the UCI campus. Rather, it's located in the city of Orange, just down the road from Disneyland. I met with Dr. Ignatius Ou, who was the oncologist running the clinical trial. I had done a quick internet search and learned Dr. Ou graduated Phi Beta Kappa from UC Berkeley, and not only earned an M.D., but a Ph.D. in molecular and cellular biology. His articles were published in the New England Journal of Medicine. There was no question I was dealing with an extraordinarily bright person.

As usual, I came armed with my laundry list of questions. These included how long did Crizotinib typically work for patients, what were the side effects, would I be able to continue to take it after the clinical trial ended, what was the cost, and what type of commitment did I need to make. I asked about TKI flares, the side effects that happen when a patient goes off these kinds of drugs. I asked if the drug would hurt my immune system. I made sure this wouldn't be a double-blind trial, where half the patients would get the drug, and half would get a sugar pill, and neither the doctor nor the patients know who gets what. I suspected I was asking more questions than a medical student would ask, although I certainly had a more vested interest in the answers.

Dr. Ou patiently answered all of my questions, but he acknowledged there were some things about the drug they did not fully know. There were some ALK patients who had been on this drug for a number of years, and the main side effects they had were some vision issues, digestive problems, and fatigue. But the drug was still fairly new, so long-term issues were unknown. He also said there were indications from their research that Crizotinib might be even more potent in treating ROS1 patients like myself than it had been in treating ALK patients. There were two dozen people in the trial, and nearly three-quarters of them were seeing a positive response to the drug. I would not need to alter my diet much, except for eliminating grapefruit, which apparently interferes with a lot of medications. He did tell me that the recommendation was to minimize alcohol use while on the drug, but I could still have a drink occasionally. Crucially, Dr. Ou assured me that everyone on the trial would get the actual drug; no one would be given a placebo.

Given his knowledge of cancer treatments, I tried to pick Dr. Ou's brain regarding a new type of treatment. Would immunotherapy be an option for me? I was intrigued with the idea behind it, that doctors would inject strains of disease into the body to trigger a reaction from the immune system. But Dr. Ou told me that although immunotherapy was working well on solid tumors, it might be problematic for me. Since my cancer had spread to the lymph nodes, some of my cancer cells were more likely to be diffuse, and immunotherapy was less apt to be effective.

If I qualified, the decision to enter the trial and to stay on the trial would be mine. He told me that while only 2 percent of lung cancer patients had the ROS1 Rearrangement, it was more common in patients who were non-smokers and who were younger, so the odds that I would qualify might be better than 2 percent. I was also lucky that we lived just a 45-minute drive away from the UCI Medical Center. Some patients on the trial did not live that close, and had to fly in regularly to participate; the next closest trial location was in Boulder, Colorado.

Finally, and most importantly, Dr. Ou told me that if the drug was effective for me, I would be able to continue to have access to it, even if the clinical trial ended. The cost of the drug would be covered by the trial, although I would need to have my health insurance pick up the cost of the periodic CT scans. I had checked with our insurance company, and the co-pays at the time were not exorbitant. It all sounded reasonable, so I signed the consent forms, and from there, they would arrange to have part of the tissue from my biopsy sent off for testing at Massachusetts General Hospital, which is the teaching hospital of Harvard Medical School.

The testing process took a good 6 weeks. In the interim, I had completed my third cycle of chemo and had gone in for CT scans to measure if any changes had taken place. The results were terrific. The tumor in my lung had been reduced in size by almost half. My first scans in March showed the tumor was 2 centimeters, which is fairly small. But in May, right before I began chemotherapy, it had grown to 3.5 centimeters, confirming that this lung cancer was aggressive and fast-moving. By early July, the chemo had shrunk the tumor back down to under 2 centimeters. The infusions were working. I was on a good path. The enemy was in retreat.

And then, on another lazy Tuesday afternoon, I received a call from Dr. Ou. He was excited to give me the good news, that I had tested positive for the ROS1 Rearrangement, and I was eligible to join the clinical trial. I could start the following month. I didn't know it at the time, but I was essentially being handed a golden ticket, a key that could possibly open the door to another decade or more of a normal life. It was the type of gift that cancer patients prayed for; I had won the lottery. I thanked Dr. Ou for calling, and I think he was very surprised when I told him I'd give the matter some thought. I'd get back to him.

11

The Toughest Decision

Today we know a lot about what Crizotinib can do; back in 2012, we did not. The clinical trial at UC Irvine was called a Phase 3 trial, which is typically the last phase prior to applying for FDA approval. The process had really begun years earlier. Once a drug has shown effectiveness in a lab setting, usually among rats or mice, it can be moved into a Phase 1 trial. This is where the drug is first tested on human patients, not just for effectiveness, but to pinpoint the optimum dosage level, one that balances efficacy with the ability to tolerate any nasty side effects.

The primary goal of a Phase 1 trial is to test the safety of the drug on humans, and this phase carries the most risk. The types of patients who enter a trial in this phase are the true pioneers. They are also the most desperate. These are patients who have often exhausted other treatments and are willing to be among the first to try something new. A few want to be on the leading edge of science. But most have simply have run out of options.

If the new drug is found to be safe, it moves into Phase 2, where the goal is to see if the drug works on specific types of cancers. Patients in a Phase 2 trial typically all get the same dose. More patients are normally in a Phase 2 trial, so there's greater opportunity to learn about side effects. If enough patients benefit from the treatment, and the side effects aren't bad, the drug moves into the next phase.

A Phase 3 clinical trial compares the effectiveness of the new drug with other treatments that have already been approved. If the new drug is found to be either more effective or safer than current treatments, it is submitted to the FDA for approval. If approved, this new drug will now become the standard of care against which other new drugs are then measured.

There is also another step called Phase 4, and this is where the FDA watches the drug over an extended period to see if there are additional side effects not previously noted. They also observe if patients are able to live longer on the drug.

As I mentioned earlier, in some clinical trials, half the patients get placebos, or sugar pills, rather than the drug itself. Those patients are part of what's called a control group, against which the patients receiving the real drug are compared. This type of clinical trial is rare for cancer drugs, in part because the main goal is to simply measure tumor shrinkage while on the drug, and in part because no patient in their right mind would ever agree to participate. When you're faced with a terminal illness, time is a precious commodity, and seeking out treatments that could save, or even extend life becomes the driving factor.

After learning I'd been accepted into the Crizotinib trial, my first inclination was to consult with other patients on the internet, which is of course, not the best protocol to follow. But other patients were good at raising issues to consider. One that was particularly thought-provoking had to do with limiting the number of clinical trials a patient enters. If I entered too many trials over time, it might eventually render me as an unacceptable candidate going forward. Certain trials prefer "fresh" participants, whose histories are not clouded by a variety of past treatments that might have impacted their immune system, or that adversely affected the body in some way. This might make the new drug appear to be less effective, and could, in turn, stymie my ability to join a trial for a true breakthrough drug that might work incredibly well for me.

On the other hand, I was also urged to not wait until all of the currently available treatment options were exhausted, as time was not on my side. The vexing part about this was not knowing which new drugs would work on me and which would not. To a certain extent, I needed to view some of these trials with a jaundiced eye. There were clinical trials experimenting on everything from stem cells to acetaminophen, and it seemed like a lot of them were just crapshoots. At this point, what I really needed was to hear from the experts.

I went in and spoke with Dr. Lieber about this. He said there was no clear answer. I reminded him of his comment, that it was better to take a pill than to do chemo, but he pointed out that this pill was not yet FDA-approved for the ROS1 Rearrangement I had; the trial was still an experiment. He consulted with his lung cancer expert, and their recommendation was that because the chemo was so effective on me, and I was tolerating the side effects well, it was advisable that I stay on chemo. But Dr. Lieber also told me he would support me in whatever direction I wanted to go. One thing I could not do was stay on chemo if I entered the clinical trial; I would not be allowed to do both. I had to choose one or the other.

Cousin Paul asked a lung cancer specialist he knew about this, and was told he was unaware of any case of a patient switching from a chemo triplet that was working well to going onto Crizotinib – but he did say there had been cases of patients with the EGFR mutation who had switched to Tarceva after going through chemo, and had success with the new drug. He thought the clinical trial would be the best path for me. So I had two different lung cancer experts suggesting two different courses of treatment. Thus, the practical question of what I should do next remained unanswered. And so I did what I had always fallen back on. I kept asking questions. And the best person to ask would naturally be another lung cancer specialist. I went back to see Dr. Ronald Natale at Cedars-Sinai.

Dr. Natale said his initial concern was that if I went onto Crizotinib now, with my tumors having shrunk on chemo, there was no way to know if my ongoing success would be due to the Crizotinib. That meant, if the tumors stayed small, it might be due to the chemo's efficacy, rather than the Crizotinib keeping them stable. It could make the Crizotinib seem effective, regardless of whether that was really the case. I appreciated Dr. Natale's concern for the integrity of the clinical trial, but my concerns were far more selfish: I wanted the treatment that would be most effective for me.

As was my custom, I peppered Dr. Natale with a lot of questions. He answered as best he could, but he avoided giving a direct response to my question as to whether I should switch from chemo to the clinical trial. I tried saying "If I were your brother, what would you recommend?" which I regret in retrospect, because there was always the chance that a doctor didn't really like his brother. But after a while, I sensed he was becoming weary of hearing me ask the same question in different ways. In the business world, one reason negotiations often reach agreement is because the parties get worn down and are tired. That may or may not have been the case here, but what happened next is Dr. Natale gave me the response I was looking for.

"Look," he said, "we know what chemo is capable of achieving, and while some patients stay on it for years, chemo is not a cure for cancer. We don't know what Crizotinib is yet. It's an unknown, especially in ROS1 patients. We can't be certain, but it might be a better long-term treatment."

And there was the answer I was after, because it provided me with exactly what I needed at that moment. Crizotinib provided hope. The clinical trial provided hope. And at that moment, there was no better feeling than having hope.

I called Dr. Ou back and told him I'd like to join the trial. He told me that in the beginning, he would need to see me every few weeks, and I would need to be tested regularly, using CT scans and blood tests. I then began to think of the time I'd need to take off from work. But as it turned out, there was another plan taking shape at the office, one being hatched behind the scenes. Carving out some free time in my schedule would soon pose no problems. Having enough free time would be the least of my concerns.

12

My Performance Review

It is a tricky business to work for a large organization. Decisions do not always make sense. Just like doctors, executives are human; they can make smart moves and they can also make mistakes. When my division head first joined DirecTV, one of his first actions was to promote me to head up the marketing research team. At that point, I had a great opportunity to build a department. I hired three managers, Wendy, Dan, and Sashi, and we formed an outstanding group that accomplished a lot. I respected my crew as more than just terrific workers -- they were great people as well. It was nice to be able to help them develop their skills and move them forward in their careers.

Years later, I unfortunately made the mistake of assuming other people would turn out to be employees that were as wonderful as Dan, Wendy, and Sashi. As our department expanded, I hired a succession of people who had good skills but not good work habits. They were not very motivated or simply didn't want to listen to anyone else's direction. But I was very fortunate to have the three I liked with me in 2008, when we had so much trouble selling our home. It was a rough time, and I'm glad I had them there to help pick up the load, when I was trying to fight off depression.

A very telling moment happened in the middle of 2008, before my life got turned upside down by our real estate fiasco. Wendy had been doing an exceptionally good job, and I recommended she be promoted. I went around and around with Sebastian, who kept coming up with delaying tactics. I knew him well enough to never try and suggest a promotion for myself, but I was also aware that there were subtle ways to put the thought in front of him, which is to say, let him be the one to come up with the idea. He was one of those people for whom you had to bury the bone and then let him find it.

At the beginning of 2009, DirecTV's entire sales and marketing department went down to Long Beach for an off-site meeting for a few days. Various executives stood up and made presentations, and one senior vice president was discussing the development of our new website. She called out myself and Wendy as being great partners in helping to test out the site among our customers, which was nice. I was in the middle of trying to sell our old home, so I was physically present, but mostly distracted during the meeting.

The following week, I sat down with Sebastian and reminded him of the very public compliment which that senior vice president had given us, and then I casually added that there were others in the company who were at a higher level than Wendy and yet contributed less. I mentioned that promotions seemed hard to come by in our department, and added that it had been a number of years since I had been promoted.

Sebastian did not respond to this directly, but I could tell it had sunk in. And about a month later he called me into his office to tell me the good news. Wendy's promotion had been approved, and oh, by the way, he decided to promote me as well. This had been during a period of months where I felt largely immobilized, had accomplished very little, was overly consumed with buying and selling our homes. My contributions to the company were at best scant, and more likely non-existent. I then received a promotion, and with it came a big raise in pay. As I said, decisions in large organizations do not always make sense. There had been times when I knew I was doing great work, yet did not get recognized or rewarded. Decisions aren't always fair. But I certainly wasn't going to quibble with this one.

Over the years, my job at DirecTV had evolved. When I first came on board in 1999, the company was growing exponentially. They were introducing new products like TiVo, developing a new remote control, launching numerous marketing and advertising programs; they needed someone with my skills to do consumer research and help test all these things out. Working at DirecTV was fun back then. I was enjoying being able to travel around the country, but the downside was that Matthew was very young, and I missed spending a lot of evenings with him.

Over time, my job changed, as the company changed. As DirecTV moved from growth mode into a mature stage in its lifecycle, there was less of a need to introduce new products and acquisition programs, and more of a need to retain customers and cut costs. My job as a market researcher shifted to evaluating our customer service and asking customers to fill out those monotonous satisfaction surveys that are now a tired bedrock of our society. They weren't so great back then, either.

In my new role, I spearheaded a program of collecting thousands of mini-surveys, evaluating call center reps and technicians that came to customers' homes to install or repair service. These evaluations were tracked carefully, and every uptick and tiny decline was analyzed *ad nauseum*. Fewer new customers were coming to DIRECTV then, and there was less emphasis on doing research about how to grow the business. Now it was more about keeping existing customers, and my role transitioned away from uncovering useful consumer insights. Instead, I came up with numbers that were simply fed into spreadsheets and PowerPoint charts. I was clearly unhappy about how my role had changed. But the income I was earning was lucrative, and I had arrived at a point in my career where I sensed this might be as good as it was going to get.

So I tolerated the tedium and settled into being comfortably shackled by a set of golden handcuffs. It made no financial sense to look for another job since I knew I was unlikely to find anything that paid close to what I was earning at DIRECTV – and certainly not without the long hours and increased pressure that often comes with joining a new company at a higher level position. I had a cushy job and could provide nicely for my family. There was no point in blowing that up just because I was a little bored.

But then 2012 arrived. Shortly after I told Sebastian about my cancer diagnosis, things began to deteriorate. Sebastian became distant and stopped including me in meetings. It almost felt like he believed my cancer was contagious. In July, he blew up at me over a relatively minor incident, began yelling at me in his office, and told me we were going to set up a time to talk about "options." This came out of the blue. He set up a meeting to review my performance the following week, and a few minutes before we were to meet, he walked into my office.

"David," he said, "we've known each other for years, and I think I need to be upfront with you and let you know I've invited someone from human resources to join us at your performance review."

I sighed. It is rarely a good sign whenever HR is involved in anything. Human Resources is there to protect the company. Their main job is to streamline the process of hiring, firing, and administering benefits. I needed to speak with someone in HR a few months earlier to discuss taking time off due to my cancer treatment. They spouted the same line as Sebastian had, that your health is the most important thing. They laid out what was involved in taking a leave of absence under the Family and Medical Leave Act. In retrospect, if I had a chance to do this all over again, I probably wouldn't have said anything to anyone at work about my cancer.

We like to hear stories of how some companies stand by their employees when they get sick, and these are indeed heartwarming tales. They are also, I believe, the exception. In my experience, companies do not want sick people around, and they don't want old people around. Old is a relative term, but in the business world, a person in their 50s is considered old. And work performance is usually lower when an employee needs to be out of the office frequently, and we also cost the company money when it comes to providing health care. I knew I faced a double whammy. I was 55 and I had cancer. My value to the company had diminished.

At our meeting, Sebastian gave me a terrible performance review. It was the worst performance review I had ever received in my entire career. In over a decade at DirecTV, I had always received very good reviews about my work. Aside from that one period, for a few months in 2008 when I struggled with depression and was unable to be effective, I had always worked hard and contributed to the company's success. As Sebastian droned on, I felt as if he was describing someone else, not me. I sat silently listening to it, feeling like debating him on each point, but clearly sensing that would be futile. He finished by telling me of the need to establish a "performance improvement plan," and he asked the HR person to go over what was involved. After she finished, Sebastian turned to me again.

"David, I have to be honest with you. This is going to be tough for you to overcome. But because you've worked here for so many years, we'd like to offer you a severance package."

And at that point, everything became crystal clear. I was being let go; the only question was did I want to leave now and get some money, or did I want to stick it out and get nothing. I listened to the HR person explain the severance package, which did contain a significant amount of money, but it was far from enough to retire on. Severance packages served to provide a smooth transition so an employee would have the funds to stay afloat while they looked for a new job. They also served to limit the number of wrongful termination lawsuits that were bound to pop up. Accepting a severance package involved signing an agreement to not sue the employer.

At the end of the meeting, which came late on a Friday morning, Sebastian suggested I take the rest of the day off and use the weekend to think about what we had discussed. I returned to my office, initially planning to begin writing a performance improvement plan, but literally gave up after five minutes. I knew this was the end. When companies want you gone, you're gone; the only question was how messy the process would be.

I also considered a change that I knew was about to happen. The company had rented space in an adjacent office building, and my team would be relocating there in a few months. I'd had a chance to review the designers' plans and saw that my new office walls would be all glass. I'd be in full view of everyone else on the floor. No more taking naps in the afternoon, which had literally provided me with a crucial means of making it through the day. Just getting 20 or 30 minutes of rest was enough to rejuvenate me and let me be productive for the rest of the day, but I knew it would never be perceived in that manner. Most employers frown on that. The corporate world is always changing, but not always for the better. For me, this small change in office architecture would add a large helping of misery, and I was not looking forward to it. But I would no longer need to worry about this. I'd soon be taking my naps at home.

Following my meeting with Sebastian and HR, I left the office in a daze. I went over to a little Mexican restaurant I loved in Manhattan Beach, a hole-in-the-wall joint called El Tarasco. It was a place for great comfort food. I stuffed myself with a huge burrito and chips, hoping that treat would help me feel better. It did, but only for a few minutes. I went for a walk on the beach, and despite the backdrop of a bright blue sky and soft ocean waves lapping the sand, I felt miserable. I was in shock. This was the same feeling I had when I was first diagnosed, and just like that time, I could sense how easy it could be to fall into a depression. It is terrible to receive a bad medical diagnosis. It is even worse to then lose your job a few months later. Clearly, 2012 was turning out to be one rotten year for me.

I finally walked back to my car and drove home. I sat down and turned on the TV. The summer Olympics, in London, were starting, and the Olympics were something I had always loved watching, and always looked forward to. But I could barely focus on it, my mind wandering away from the games, and back to my own precarious situation. Around 4:00 p.m., Andrea walked in. She noted I was home early. She asked if everything was okay.

"No," I told her. It was not okay. It most certainly was not.

13

Weighing The Package

There are plenty of wrongful termination lawsuits brought against employers these days. Most are unsuccessful.

About a year before losing my job, I had watched a documentary called *Hot Coffee*. The movie gets its name from the famous case in which a woman sued McDonald's because a cup of coffee she purchased ended up spilling on her and burning her legs. But a big part of the film detailed how corporations have created a system that protects their business interests and makes it difficult for individuals who take legal action against them. The film breathed life into an otherwise boring subject called tort reform, which, among other things, strives to take power away from juries and hand it to arbitrators, who are often much more sympathetic to the plight of the corporation.

When an employee is hired now, they are frequently asked to sign an agreement stating that if they ever file a lawsuit against the company, it goes to binding arbitration. The employee thus forfeits their right to a jury trial, and the case is decided by an arbitrator, who is often a retired judge. And unlike individual employees, large corporations are obviously involved in more wrongful termination suits, so arbitrators do not want to alienate employers. In the selection process of arbitrators, employers know which arbitrators are inclined to rule for the big companies and which are not. So, unless something truly egregious has occurred, and there is verifiable proof of discrimination, it's in the arbitrator's best interest to side with the corporation.

I had seen firsthand what this process was like. DirecTV had been sued by a former employee for wrongful termination, and the burden of proof seemed to clearly be on the back of the former employee. The process was long and arduous, and it struck me as very difficult to prove discrimination without providing substantial concrete evidence. In the end, the arbitrator in that case ruled for DirecTV, and the former employee received nothing.

After I told Andrea about what had transpired earlier that day, she was furious and insisted we see an attorney. She was outraged and could not believe the company would dare show me the door just a few months after learning I had cancer. She wanted to fight an injustice, and she wanted to see them pay for the way they were mistreating me. But I was reluctant to go forward with legal action for a number of critical reasons, and my rationale was only partly due to our unlikely chance of winning.

My situation was tenuous. I had just been diagnosed with terminal cancer, and despite the encouraging results from the chemotherapy, and being admitted to the clinical trial, there was no guarantee of long-term remission. My 5-year life expectancy, even if it were much better than 10 percent, was still not terrific. And to get those extra years, I felt I'd need to summon my energies on overcoming the physical, mental, and emotional toll of fighting cancer.

To cover our bases, we did speak with an attorney who specialized in employment law. He reviewed my situation and told me that yes, we did have a case, but he warned me about another tactic we might encounter. Plaintiffs in my situation, who had serious mortality issues, were more likely to see the employer use delaying tactics to extend the case for as long as possible. This was straight out of the tobacco companies' playbook, to push hearings out for years, in the hope that the plaintiff died before the case was heard. Given my life expectancy, there was every reason to expect this tactic to be utilized here, and if I did die before the arbitrator was able to rule, the case would be over, and my family would get nothing. The attorney reviewed the severance package the company offered me, and he said while it was not abundant, it was reasonably good, and better than other packages he had seen. For me, this was a green light to move forward and accept the package.

One of my biggest concerns, though, was maintaining good health insurance. But doing so at an affordable cost was becoming more and more challenging. When I first began my career, health insurance was included as an employee benefit, often at no cost to the employee. After reaching a small deductible, usually $100, the insurance would pick up 80 percent of all costs. That sounds nostalgic now, as modern health insurance plans can include sky-high deductibles of thousands of dollars a year, and employees are now required to contribute a lot to the premiums. The choice of doctors is often limited to those in a particular network.

Many years ago, I worked for a company that offered an interesting choice of health plans. One plan would actually *pay me* $50 a month, rather than me having to pay a premium. The downside was a huge deductible, one I would likely meet only if I were hospitalized. I was in my late 20s, and in good health, so I figured this would be all right for me. What happened during that year, however, was that I became reluctant to go see a doctor when I had any sort of an ailment. And of course, that was the year I had numerous maladies. From lingering colds to a plantar wart on my foot, to a sprained wrist playing basketball, I toughed it out rather than see a doctor. By the end of that year, I had learned my lesson – good health insurance is worth the cost.

What constitutes good insurance these days comes at a very high price. If I took the severance package, I would be eligible for COBRA, which means I could maintain the same corporate health insurance coverage I had as a DirecTV employee. The only difference is I would be responsible for paying the full premium. It's only an employee benefit when you are actually an employee. The cost for me at the time was $12,000 a year, which was by no means cheap. The general idea of COBRA though, is that it provides a bridge until you can find a new job, and your new employer can then provide health coverage. That was the idea, anyway. Over the next few years, our family's health insurance premiums would more than double.

During this time, I started to meet with more friends and colleagues to discuss not only my cancer diagnosis, but leaving my job. One woman I had worked with for many years suggested that my division head might not have had much of a choice in ushering me out of the company. It was entirely possible he was just doing the dirty work that someone high up in human resources was pushing him to do.

Many corporations are self-insured when it comes to providing employee health insurance, and they contract with companies like Blue Cross and Blue Shield as third-party administrators. So it might seem as if the insurance company was handling things, but, in fact, it was the large employer who covered the cost of health care. At the time of my departure, I was still on chemotherapy, and I suspected an employee requiring expensive cancer treatments like this would be perceived as a financial burden. In the end, however, this was all conjecture. I would never truly know what happened. Big companies are good at remaining tight-lipped.

If there is a key to life, I believe it lies in forgiveness. A few years ago, someone told me a story about a friend of theirs, whose girlfriend cheated on him. Those close to him were furious and encouraged the man to break up with her. But after lots of long talks, he chose to forgive her, and he stayed in the relationship. He summed it up by saying he was doing what he wanted to do. If he had broken up with her, he'd be doing what other people wanted him to do. And such is the path to forgiveness. It is often easier for the person who has been wronged to forgive and move on. It is not so easy for those close to that person. They only see one side. They were not privy to the long, tearful conversations that transpired, nor were they so easy to forgive what they considered a betrayal. They are the ones who hold grudges. They want the guilty party to pay.

I left DirecTV after spending exactly 13 years with them. In the end, I looked back on my time there fondly. It was one of the best periods of my career. Our research contributed to the company's growth, and I flourished professionally. I made a lot of friends. My time there did not end well, and it did not end the way I'd have preferred. But it did end, and I needed to move forward.

Spending decades with one employer, retiring at age 65, and sailing into a blissful retirement are sadly anachronisms. I could have sued, and I might have won, but I also might have lost, and wasted a lot of time and energy doing so. I did not feel like fighting wars on multiple fronts, and my war with cancer needed to take precedence. I had to close this chapter of my career. So, after a lot of discussions, we decided to accept the severance package. It did not mean I would never work again. It just meant I would never work for DirecTV again.

14

The Miracle Drug

At the start of 2012, before all of the drama surrounding my cancer emerged, Andrea and I had planned to take a week during the summer and visit Alaska. We had not anticipated that I'd be newly unemployed, but we finally decided to just go on living our lives for the time being. My final day at DirecTV came a week before we flew to Anchorage and took a cruise down to Vancouver. It seemed like a good way to begin a new chapter, immersing ourselves in a totally different environment. And unlike where I was during our silent drive through Arizona, I had had five months to think about my situation. I was neither a doctor nor a seer, and I couldn't predict how long these treatments would work for me. But I did have a plan I was developing.

In the corporate world, most companies craft a mission statement. This is to help guide the business, and in a healthy culture, many decisions flow from having a primary purpose. The mission statement clarifies what the business wants to achieve, and can serve as a guidepost when challenges arise. But it mostly serves to encapsulate the core values that define the essence of what the company is all about.

It occurred to me that every cancer patient has their own unique mission, too. Some want to live life to the fullest, even if it means a shorter life. Others want to extend their life as long as possible, regardless of the painful treatments they may need to endure. I decided my mission was to live as normal a life as I could, for as long as I could. My plan to get there was to exhaust all options in support of that mission. As I thought this through, it continued to make sense for me to enter the clinical trial for Crizotinib. It offered the best shot at a normal life, coupled with the possibility of a longer life. Being on chemo was not a normal way of living, not with toxins being dripped into my arm every three weeks. I also thought back to what Dr. Natale had told me:

"Chemo is not a cure for cancer. We don't know what Crizotinib is yet."

The words resonated with me and snuck up on me at times during our Alaska trip. Although we were 3,000 miles from home, the issues from home stayed with me. Alaska, even in the heart of summer, is mostly cold and gray. The days were overcast, and the temperature rarely inched above 60 degrees. It reminded me of the depressing aspects of early spring in upstate New York, where I had gone to college.

In Alaska, the glaciers were stunning, and we saw lots of wildlife. And even though cancer was never too far from my mind, being in a different place for a week was very therapeutic. Oddly, at one point, someone on our cruise organized what they called a "cancer hike," which was no more than a bunch of us doing circuits walking around the ship. At the start, the leader asked how many cancer survivors there were, and a dozen of us raised our hands. He asked each to say how long they had survived cancer. When it was my turn, I said, "one month," because that was when results from my CT scan showed the tumors shrinking in size. That comment got the biggest round of applause.

After we returned home, I started getting ready for the clinical trial. I had my sixth and final chemotherapy cycle, and it was by far the most grueling. Chemo has a cumulative effect on patients. The first three or four infusions were tolerable, but the final ones exacted their toll. Whereas it had taken me a day or two to recover from the initial infusions, the final cycle took over a week for me to overcome. I was fatigued and achy, and the thought of most food made my stomach churn. In many ways, I was glad to be at home and not dealing with the day-to-day grind of a demanding job. The following Sunday afternoon we took Matthew to see *The Three Stooges* movie, and there was a scene where they showed the Stooges as children. Larry, the one with the thinning hair, was pointed out by an adult in the scene, who thought he was losing his hair because of a cancer treatment.

"How long's the kid got?" the adult asked. "He's taking chemo, right?"

At that point, I had to lean over to Matthew and whisper to him, "That's not how it's going to be for me." He just laughed and said he knew. Thankfully, he was starting to gain some optimism, too.

Before entering the clinical trial, I had another set of CT scans done, and they revealed that my tumors had now shrunk by more than 70 percent since starting chemo. I had to go through a "washout period," which meant being off chemo for a month before starting on Crizotinib. This would ensure my results going forward could be viewed as directly resulting from the Crizotinib. I also drove down to UC Irvine to be examined by an ophthalmologist. She took baseline images of my eyes, which was needed because a side effect of Crizotinib was the potential for vision problems.

I downed my first dose of Crizotinib in Dr. Ou's office on September 28, 2012. Andrea and I stayed there for a few hours to make sure there weren't any immediate reactions, and there were none. So, furnished with a one-month supply of pills, to be taken twice a day, I began the regiment. I barely felt any ill effects from the drug. Unlike with chemo, I had no digestive issues and no stomach distress.

Over time, though, I did develop some odd side effects. In addition to significant fatigue, I observed swelling in my feet, ankles, and calves. I also noticed that my right hand had become freakishly bigger than my left hand. It wasn't a problem, other than just looking very strange. The area under my toes had become numb, and my hands were often cold. I also understood the reason Dr. Ou was concerned about my vision. When going from a dimly lit room to a brightly lit one, I would often see a swirl of colors for a few seconds. It wasn't a bad feeling, just a bizarre one. All of these side effects seemed tolerable. If this was the cost of gaining a few extra years, it would be an easy price to pay.

As part of the clinical trial requirements, there would be a blood test every month, and CT scans every two months, followed by visits to Dr. Ou to monitor results, and make sure there were no adverse reactions to the drug. At one point, I called Cousin Paul, whom I seemed to be using as an impartial arbiter, to ask about the radiation involved in doing this many CT scans. I had heard that large doses of radiation could cause cancer, another artifact of using the internet as a fountain of knowledge. That these scans which monitored my response to a life-saving drug could, potentially, cause cancer in and of itself, was a little ironic, but also nerve-wracking. Paul told me it was technically possible, but the odds were low. He also said I had bigger fish to fry.

The CT scans quickly became routine, although they invariably created a long day for me. I had developed high creatinine levels, which meant my kidneys were not functioning properly. High creatinine levels were a side effect of Crizotinib, but not a common one. Breathing issues, vision problems, fatigue, and digestive issues dominated the exhaustive list of what could afflict patients taking the drug. There had also been isolated reports of a few more serious side effects, which included low blood sugar, reduced heart rate, and problems with the liver. But not every patient experienced these, and realistically, none of these issues would have stopped me from taking Crizotinib. It offered me the best shot at having a longer life, even if it meant a few, ahem, inconveniences. And though my creatinine levels were elevated, I did not feel any adverse physical symptoms. The results of the blood test were more of a warning sign and a signal for the doctor to take an extra step during scans.

In doing CT scans every two months, the technician was required to use IV contrast to highlight the areas of the body being tested, which would more accurately measure any change in the size of the tumors. The contrast itself was iodine-based and went directly into my veins during the scans. To help my body handle the contrast, Dr. Ou suggested I receive hydration first, which meant having a saline solution drip into my veins for two hours before each scan. The scans themselves only took a few minutes to complete, but I often had to wait an hour to get into the scanning room, plus wait another hour to get the disk to take down to Dr. Ou. All this took half a day or more, but not having a job meant I could take all the time I needed. This was the first time in decades that I had had so much freedom. While I missed my regular paycheck, I didn't miss being in endless meetings, or needing to calm an anxious executive about how our surveys were going.

But this period in my life was hardly stress-free. Every CT scan brought with it a phenomenon called *scanxiety*, waiting on pins and needles for the results. Before I left DirecTV, I started seeing a psychiatrist. The stress of dealing with cancer had been gnawing at me, and I needed to talk with someone. I asked around and was referred to a doctor in Brentwood who specialized in working with patients diagnosed with serious illnesses. This doctor also took insurance. On the surface, he sounded like the right guy for me.

My first visit was pleasant enough; he struck me as a kindly man in his early 70s. He asked me about my situation, and I said my concerns centered on Andrea and Matthew, and how they would deal with my potentially not being around. Which is to say I needed to deal with my own fears, part of which were financial. We had been putting away money for Matthew's college tuition, but we had a ways to go. We still had a mortgage to make payments on, and my life insurance money would only go so far.

More than that though, the experience I had with my brother Jeffrey's death was the one weighing heaviest on my mind. There was a mourning period, and then people moved on with their lives. Jeffrey became a memory, one I watched fade over time. I didn't want to be forgotten, but I also didn't want

Matthew to view himself as the boy whose father died too young. I was trying to work through these emotions, and not getting anywhere on my own. I tried to stay positive, but I would sometimes look up at the sky and wonder if I would be up there soon. I knew this was not good.

These talks started out as helpful and therapeutic, but over the next few months, I began to notice something different about our sessions. I had been in treatment with a few psychologists over the years, some of these sessions had been helpful, others had been a waste of time, but I knew the basic protocol. There were dos and don'ts.

My new psychiatrist would, at times, interject with his political views. When I discussed my concerns about Matthew entering adulthood without a father, he would boast about the idyllic childhood his grandkids were enjoying. When I talked about the complicated relationship I had with my father, he would hijack the conversation and tell me how great life had been for him when he was growing up. This struck me as unsettling. I didn't think therapists were supposed to be sharing their own history in this way. This was supposed to be my time, to discuss my issues, to deal with my problems, not an opportunity for the therapist to reflect on his.

I finally mentioned this to Andrea, and as a psychotherapist, she was appalled. Andrea's father had been a psychiatrist, and a number of other family members worked in this field. What I sensed was inappropriate, she confirmed as a breach of professional conduct. I needed to discuss my own situation, and instead, I was listening to someone prattle on about theirs. The final straw came when the psychiatrist began making fun of Dr. Ou's name. Here was someone trying to save my life, and I had to listen to this therapist spew nonsense. My 13-year-old son had more maturity. I finally told the doctor I was ending our sessions, that they had ceased to be productive. It was yet another insight that just because someone held the title of doctor, it didn't always mean they were going to be helpful.

Separating from this "doctor" was necessary, but I still needed an outlet to deal with the tedious aspects of my situation, and to find a way to air my emotions. I was feeling a great deal of sadness since my diagnosis, and I knew that this needed to be dealt with somehow.

Shortly after I stopped seeing this psychiatrist, I found a gig that ultimately evolved into an extraordinary outlet. I was able to get my feelings out in a highly productive way, and it also turned into a side hustle that, surprisingly, became somewhat lucrative as well. It was all so unexpected, and it literally fell into my lap.

15

When One Door Closes

I have always enjoyed writing. I like telling stories, and my dream career was to be a novelist. I started writing my first novel when I was 9 years old, a war story, which was ridiculous of course, since all I knew about war was what I'd learned by watching TV. I wrote myself into a corner after three pages. At age 16, I managed to write two chapters of a novel about a degenerate gambler. I obviously needed some real-world experiences, but at least the simple act of putting pen to paper was a step in the right direction.

In college, I took a number of writing classes and became more capable at the art of storytelling. I was concerned, however, that it would take me many years to develop a career in fiction writing. My parents were pressuring me to major in a subject that would help me earn a living, so I reluctantly put novel writing aside for more practical pursuits. I called it relinquishing the dream; they called it growing up.

As I entered the working world, I decided I would write in my spare time. But I didn't have the drive to put in the time needed to hone my craft — and to also be able to enjoy life in my off hours. This all came to a head when I turned 30. I was frustrated that my business career was not taking off, and I regretted giving up my dream too quickly. In a fit of pique, I quit my job and vowed to dedicate a year to being a full-time author, renting a cheap, rent-controlled apartment, and cutting expenses.

I wrote a long literary novel, which was largely terrible, but I did accomplish some significant goals. I learned how to build an engaging, albeit disjointed plot, develop a few compelling characters, and most importantly, to write and complete a full novel. That it was unpublishable was immaterial; most first novels are not very good. After that, I wrote a mystery featuring a private investigator modeled after protagonists created by the likes of Raymond Chandler and Robert B. Parker. It was called *Post Pattern*, named after a football play. The first literary agent who read it told me they loved it, and took me on as a client. I wrote a follow-up novel in the same genre, with the same main character. I was on my way to a bright new career. Or so I thought.

The feedback my agent began getting from publishers was that *Post Pattern* was well-written, but not distinctive. One publisher felt I was trying to drop a 1940s Philip Marlowe-style detective into modern-day Los Angeles, and it didn't feel right. Others said there wasn't anything sufficiently unique about my main character, Burnside, a former USC football player-turned-LAPD officer, turned private investigator. They cited mystery writers who crafted main characters who were Native American, women, people of color, disabled, or suffering from a particular malady. They all had an unusual characteristic or challenge that set them apart. Burnside had none of these. *Post Pattern* was just well-written, and apparently, well-written was not a compelling reason for anyone to publish it. I entered a contest run by St. Martin's Press for first-time mystery authors, and my book won third prize. The first prize was getting published. I can't recall what the second prize was, but all I received was a nice letter. After a couple of years of actively pursuing this dream of being a published author, I reluctantly gave it up again and re-focused on a business career. At least the money was good.

In early 1993, I landed a job as marketing research manager with Disney Channel. Later that year I met Andrea, and we were married a few years after that. We had Matthew soon after we got married, and I quickly fell into being a suburban family man, going to work every day, coming home each night. We bought a small house. It was a nice lifestyle, and I was comfortable. I recognized I did not have a creative outlet, but I also didn't miss the ongoing anxiety of trying to attract a publisher. As enjoyable as writing could be, it was also frustrating at times, when the creative juices were stymied and not flowing. A business career was steadier. It paid consistently. I knew that not everyone fulfilled their aspirations, but that was becoming okay. What I had was good. I traveled for business and got to see a lot of the country, and enjoyed most of it. I survived a torturous home sale in the middle of a global financial crisis. I lost a lot in 2012 – my health, my job, and my income – but I did not lose my way. And as the saying goes, when one door closes, another one opens.

In the fall of 2012, Andrea and I went to Matthew's middle school one night for a parent-teacher conference. We met with Alex Cussen, Matthew's 8th grade English teacher, and during the course of our conversation, he mentioned he had just published a novel as an independent author. My interest was piqued. He told me that when Amazon introduced the Kindle e-reader, they allowed authors to self-publish on their site. He said it was fairly easy to do. I looked into it, and a light bulb went off. There were lots of self-published novels on Amazon, with authors essentially running their own publishing houses. The author had final say on everything about their book, from the content in the final manuscript, down to the style of fonts used. The author arranged for and approved the cover art, as well as did all the marketing and promotion. The author was the chief executive officer of their own business, that of selling books. And it occurred to me that maybe, just maybe, I could do this, too.

I dug up a copy of *Post Pattern* and read it again. I thought it held up pretty well after 20 years, but it clearly needed updating. No one used answering machines or faxes anymore. The Mazda RX-7 had been retired. Some of the urban slang had changed. I spent my days rewriting the book, polishing it, and making it appropriate for the 21st century. I formed my own publishing company. I had Andrea and Matthew read the novel, and I asked a friend with an editorial background to go through it as well. I tried hiring a cover artist but disliked what she came up with, so I created my own book cover, doing what experts say you should not do, which is to use a vacation photo. I used a sunset photo I'd taken on a trip to Hawaii a few years earlier. Interestingly, that cover won a number of awards, so go figure.

Post Pattern was published in February 2013. I had considered sending it around again to literary agents, but ultimately decided against it. I didn't have a year to wait and see if a publishing house would bite, nor did I want to battle with editors over details of the book. I wanted this to be mine. And in reading up on becoming an independent author, it struck me that this was absolutely possible. I learned there were some authors earning six-figure incomes on their own, and they didn't have to share the proceeds with anyone other than Amazon.

My marketing plan began with creating a list of email addresses of everyone I had ever met, and even some I had not. I went through my LinkedIn connections, added friends and family and any colleagues I had ever come into contact with. I sent around email announcements about my venture and encouraged everyone to buy a copy of *Post Pattern.* Many did. After a few weeks, I was getting a good number of sales, but then things slowed. You only have so many friends and family.

I began trying to promote the book by advertising on Amazon and Facebook, but I quickly discovered the key to making money as an independent author was developing a series. Entice readers to buy the first book in the series and get them hooked on the main character. If they enjoyed reading the first one, they were likely to buy the rest of the series. I read that Martin Scorsese believed that the job of an artist was to get your audience to care about your obsessions. So I went back and dug up a second Burnside book I had written two decades earlier, previously titled *Second Chance*, and rewrote that one, too.

Imitation is not only the best sort of flattery, but it is also the easiest way to create a workable template. Research what others have done, and see if what they did can be replicated. In looking at the works of successful mystery writers, I discovered many had created a theme for their titles. John D. MacDonald used a color in the title of each of his Travis McGee books. Sue Grafton had created the Alphabet series, with her *A Is For Alibi, B Is For Burglar*, etc. Since my first two books had a football theme, I changed the title of the second book to *Fade Route*, another football play, and I published it in September of 2013.

Then came the trickiest part – writing the next one, because the first two books had been written decades ago. Surprisingly, the words flowed effortlessly. I already had an established protagonist, some interesting supporting characters, and a great location in Los Angeles. I decided to craft the third Burnside book around a company that installed cable TV systems in people's homes. I had done a lot of work at DirecTV with our in-home installers, and as they say, write about what you know. The third book in the Burnside series was called *Bubble Screen*, and I released it in March 2014. I now had a bona fide mystery series of my own.

I continued to write regularly and had my system down to a science. I would spend a month developing an intricate plot, two months writing the first draft, another month editing it, and then publishing it on Amazon. I would then take a one-month breather to recharge my batteries and begin on the next book. Wash, rinse, repeat.

By 2015, I was starting to make some decent money. Again, not enough for it to be a full-time gig, but enough to pay for a few vacations, good seats at Laker games, and extra spending money. But most of all, the writing process was therapeutic. While I could never actually verbalize the snarky comments I wrote in my books, I could certainly have Burnside, my alter ego, make these cutting remarks. If someone wasn't being straight with him, Burnside would feel free to insult them, and usually with a good bit of zing.

Sometimes he would goad bad guys into a brawl and handily clobber them. All of the confrontations that would have landed me in jail if I did them in real life were now wide open for my imagination to explore and write about. As I liked to say, I'm not Burnside, but Burnside is me. Over time, I eventually wrote 13 books in the series.

After a few years, I decided I wanted to write a novel with a cancer theme. I was not yet up to the task of writing a memoir and digging painfully into my own cancer journey, but I thought if I wrapped a story of the illness around an interesting plot, I could weave in the cancer theme. I had spent a lot of time studying the 2016 presidential election and had become well-versed in the intricacies of political campaigns. I had always found them interesting. They reminded me of a sporting event, complete with combative fans, expert analysis, a boatload of statistics, and a final score.

As a survey researcher, I had a good grasp of polling, and this became a part of the story. I also went back and read up on some of the great books on presidential campaigns, especially the ones by Theodore H. White. So shortly after the 2016 election, I began writing a political thriller called *Curse Of The Afflicted.* The story was about a political operative, a presidential campaign manager who is diagnosed with lung cancer in the middle of his candidate's run for the White House. To add some intriguing tension, I had him get roped into an assassination attempt as well.

Curse Of The Afflicted remains one of my favorite and most important books. I think it contains some of my very best writing, but alas, it was also the book that sold the fewest number of copies. As I had learned early on, that books in a series sold well; standalone novels were much harder to develop traction. And even though I had an ongoing series and had a lot of interested readers, I was not able to get this book to take off. So I went back to writing more Burnside stories.

Around that time, I repackaged the series into boxed sets, which are three eBooks sold together at a discounted rate. These did well, and I stopped being exclusive to Amazon for a while so I could begin selling through online retailers such as Barnes & Noble, Apple, and Kobo. In addition to expanding my audience, I was able to accomplish something else that was personally important. I applied to an online marketing agency called BookBub, which I used to promote the Burnside series. In February 2018, I ran a BookBub promotion for my first boxed set, which contained the first 3 Burnside books. During the one-week run, I sold nearly 10,000 copies of that set, earning a place on the *USA Today* Bestsellers List. I was ranked # 92, and it was an incredibly proud moment for me. Importantly, my other books also began to sell well and the next few months were a bonanza. Like everything else in life, sales eventually tapered off, but this was an exciting period, and I felt very gratified.

One of the unexpected surprises of writing books was the feedback I got from readers. At the end of each novel, I inserted a section thanking people for reading the book, and inviting them to join my mailing list, so I could alert them when the next book came out. I added well over 1,000 readers this way. Most surprising though, was the response I got when I would send out these email alerts. I would always get dozens of replies, many from readers I had never personally met. I would estimate 99 percent of the emails were extremely flattering and positive, and I answered almost every one of them. Once in a while, I would get a whiny email complaining about some minor typo or grammatical snafu, and those I just ignored.

Because I had originally created this email list from people I had come across at various junctures in my life and career, it also helped me stay in touch with people. It allowed me to keep up with old friends from New York, reconnect with my brother's best friend from his high school days, and interact with some of my teachers. A neighbor who lived in the apartment upstairs from us in New York found me on Facebook, and it turned out he was a big mystery fan. I heard from people I hadn't been in contact with for decades. It was fascinating to see how people's lives had turned out.

The entire writing and publishing process was very gratifying, but also very necessary for me. I was finally able to release a lot of pent-up creative energy and see my efforts not only entertain readers but also earn some money as well. It did not replace the comfort of a regular paycheck each week, but it was something.

My severance payout from DirecTV finally arrived, so I had money in the bank and wasn't worried in the short term. Still, I did have long-term concerns about supporting a family and paying for Matthew's college expenses, not to mention funding our own retirement, which no longer seemed so far away. Andrea's practice only brought in so much; she was effectively working part-time. I knew at some point I would need to go back to the workaday world and earn a paycheck. What I encountered next was something that surprised me, although looking back on it, I really should not have been surprised at all. All of the warning signs were there.

16

Re-entering the Work Force

Ageism is alive and well in corporate America. Years ago, a colleague made an offhand comment that it was rare that we ever saw anyone in their 60s working in a corporation. In fact, the only ones I usually saw were at the highest levels of the company. These were senior executives, whose decades of experience were considered necessary to steer the ship, even though they might not still have the same energy as they had in their prime. But throughout the rest of many organizations, older employees were few and far between, and were usually kept on only if they had a unique skill. An aerospace engineer who was thoroughly versed in satellite technology. An I.T. expert who could work with software systems that virtually no one else could understand. A sales manager with decades of contacts built up. But these were the anomalies. Everyone else was replaceable.

In middle management, many people in their 50s have been transitioned out of companies, given a severance package, and shown the door. I think there is an assumption that younger workers have more energy, have the skills that are most in need and are more open to learning newer techniques, software, and approaches to business. The idea that it's tough to teach an old dog new tricks has some slivers of truth in there; some jobs may only be right for us during certain periods in our lives.

The first job I ever had was also the best job I ever had. I was 14 years old and began working as a vendor at Madison Square Garden. I sold peanuts, soda, and franks. I got in to see events I never could have otherwise seen. A lot of New York Knicks basketball games and Rangers hockey games were sold out, especially for the playoffs. While I had to work during much of the games, I was usually able to watch the final period, and often in a pretty good seat. I also got in to see a few Muhammed Ali boxing matches, a Rolling Stones concert, and countless Ringling Brothers circus shows. The experience also taught me something about the need to have some guile in the business world.

When I first applied at the Garden, I was turned away. In New York, you could work a job at 14, but not at night; for that, you had to be 16 years old. Since most of the events at Madison Square Garden were in the evening, this posed a problem, but one that was easy to get around. I altered the birthdate on my working papers so it read that I was 16. The same supervisor who initially rejected me did not remember who I was when I re-applied. He now accepted my application and told me I could start working right away. I thanked him, and I learned an interesting lesson. The unexpected is always possible. Don't let minor inconveniences like established rules stand in your way.

I also, unexpectedly, discovered something else. When I turned 16, my work records said I was 18, which, at the time, allowed me to sell beer. The legal age for drinking – and selling – alcohol had not yet been raised to 21. There were instances when, near the end of a game, if I had one beer left on my tray, I would simply find an empty seat, sit down, watch the game, and drink the beer. I was just 16 and had no understanding of the number of rules or laws I was breaking. And the one time I got caught drinking on the job, my boss just laughed it off and told me not to do it again. It was a more innocent time.

At the start of my senior year in high school, my father sat me down and gave me another life lesson, that of limited finances. He worked for the post office, and my mother taught at a junior high school. Together they made a decent living, but they both had government jobs, and we were not wealthy. My father told me he and my mother could afford to send me to one of the state universities in New York if I wanted to go away to college. But he also pointed out that if I wanted to go to NYU or Columbia, they could afford the tuition, but only if I lived at home. He mentioned nothing about student loans or scholarships, and I didn't know enough to ask. In the back of my mind, I thought about California. I had grown up watching USC play football against Notre Dame and UCLA, and in the Rose Bowl game for many years on New Year's Day. There was a small part of me that hoped I could find a way to Los Angeles to attend USC. That option wasn't in the cards. At least not yet.

I had the grades to get into NYU, although Columbia was a stretch. Regardless, I was sick of New York City and wanted out. Growing up in the late 1960s and early 1970s, I had seen New York evolve from a glitzy city into a bleak, crime-ridden cesspool. Riding the subway home from Madison Square Garden late at night was an unsettling experience; the trains were splattered with graffiti, and I sometimes felt unsafe. On more than one occasion, I witnessed people get held up at gunpoint. The city was revitalized in the 1990s but that was too late for me. My teenage years had been little more than a challenge to get through and escape from, rather than a time to grow and explore. It was this not-so-terrific experience that weighed heavily on my mind many years later, when we discussed with Matthew where he should go to high school.

I applied to half a dozen campuses in the State University of New York system, but SUNY Oswego, just north of Syracuse, was the first to accept me. My parents and I drove up there on a Saturday in February, and we must have lucked into one of the few gorgeous days they had that winter. It was all blue sky, puffy clouds, and temperatures in the mid-40s, brisk, but manageable. Oswego struck me as a picturesque campus situated right on the shores of

Lake Ontario, and everyone seemed to be in a good mood. Students were throwing Frisbees on the quad and walking around with happy smiles on their faces. Everyone we spoke with seemed to like it there.

As we left, I decided this was where I wanted to go to college. Even though I was subsequently accepted by other schools I applied to, I was sold on Oswego. What I later discovered was that Oswego was a beautiful place for about six months a year, largely from May through October. The other six months, beginning in November, were typically windy, overcast, frigid, and snowy. That idyllic day when we visited had been an aberration.

In terms of academics, Oswego offered a myriad of courses I was interested in. That was great, except for the fact that I couldn't figure out what I wanted to major in. There was a writing arts program, a broadcasting school, plenty of interesting social science classes, as well as a business major. I took classes in all of them and changed my major every semester. By the middle of my junior year, I was nowhere near being on track to graduate on time.

When my father told me he wouldn't support me beyond my tentative graduation date, it provided the impetus to at least get focused. I chose business administration as a major, simply because it would provide the easiest path toward getting a job after graduation. Still, I needed to take a huge course load for the final three semesters, as well as go to summer school in order to finish in time. I had no opportunity for a social life during that last year and a half, but I did learn I was capable of climbing a steep hill, one that at first seemed too big to scale. The impossible now seemed possible. Things may look tough at first, but maybe you can do it. Take it one step at a time. You just have to try.

This type of life lesson turned out to be especially helpful in my cancer treatment, many decades later, as I transitioned from chemo to Crizotinib. It was nice to be off of chemo, but a little scary to be trying an experimental drug, with lots of potential side effects. But I slowly began to feel physically better. Each day seemed better than the one before. I began to think about working again. As nice as the time off was, having a steady paycheck was nicer.

Part of my severance package included services with an outplacement company. With their help, I rebuilt my resume, polished my interviewing skills, and began networking. Most of my networking was done by phone, and I managed to get a number of interviews with some good companies. Yahoo, Auto Trader, Universal Music, and Farmers Insurance all interviewed me over the phone, and the interviews went great. I was able to show off my knowledge, demonstrate my interest, and they all seemed to like what they heard. Each of them invited me to come for an in-house interview. But from the moment I walked through the door, the good vibes I experienced on the phone were gone.

Over the years, my blond hair had turned gray, an undeniable sign of aging. For a while, I colored my hair, and I probably should have continued. But in the end, your age is your age, and it's tough to hide it. The people who sounded so excited to interview me when we were on the phone, were not so keen on hiring me. On my resume, I had clipped everything from before 1993, so it appeared I would be younger. It was slightly misleading, but that was part of the game. I thought if I could just get a face-to-face interview, I could wow them, and it would lead to a job offer. I thought wrong. At Yahoo, I felt as if I were 20 years older than every person there. Things did not end well.

The interviews did take me to some interesting places, including the offices of the Playboy Channel. Andrea shook her head when I told her I had been asked to come in for an interview, but well, a job is a job. While I was waiting in the lobby, I noticed two women, obviously models, waiting as well, albeit for a different position. I thought I could get very used to this work environment. Interestingly, the executives I spoke with were all very smart and very professional. They did ask if I had an issue with the Playboy lifestyle, and I said no. I'm a believer that, as long as no one gets hurt, people should do what they feel like doing. In the end, the job itself was more about data analytics than marketing research, and we mutually agreed that I was not an ideal candidate for that role. But it left me encouraged that there were still people who would judge me for who I am, not for how old I was. That this revelation came by way of a pay TV network showing soft porn was immaterial. You get your life's lessons where you can.

For an 18-month period, beginning in October 2012 and lasting through April 2014, I sent out countless resumes and got an occasional interview. I spoke with everyone from Amazon to Paramount Studios to the NFL Network to Vans Sneakers. Not many of these openings were ideal fits with my background. Companies these days often look for the perfect candidate, even if it means a job opening remains unfilled for months.

In one instance, a consulting firm brought me back for seven separate interviews. I agreed to go, in part, because I had nothing else to do, and their offices were in Westwood, close to our home. Years ago, I had interviewed with Disney Channel, and they also brought me in for seven interviews, culminating in a job offer, and I really loved my time working at Disney. Unfortunately, the consulting firm not only failed to make me an offer, they never even had the decency to get back to me and tell me I didn't get the job. This was how the business world worked now. Times had changed.

17

The Consulting Gig

With my job search leading me nowhere, I began to explore the possibility of starting my own consulting business. In the fall of 2013, my friend and former boss from Disney Channel, Tom Meredith, referred me to a contact of his, Patti, the head of marketing research at DISH Network. He suggested she might be a good person for me to contact. Before I spoke with her, I looked at my separation agreement with DirecTV and confirmed there was no restriction on working for a direct competitor. The only requirement was that I not reveal any trade secrets or confidential information about DirecTV.

I sent an email to Patti, and she responded quickly. Patti had recently started at DISH and was busy building a new team. I didn't bother asking about a full-time job because the company was located just outside of Denver, and I wasn't prepared to leave Los Angeles. This was before the pandemic, and before the days when working remotely was a normal option. I knew Andrea would never want to leave southern California, and a move would cause a big disruption in Matthew's life. My mother had relocated to L.A. shortly after Matthew was born. We couldn't just up and leave her in L.A., and moving a person who was in their late 80s to a new part of the country was not a good idea. I had talked to a few colleagues who commuted to a different city to work during the week, trudging to the airport early on a Monday morning and returning home on a Friday night flight. It was hectic, and it was wearisome. They were not living great lives.

I met Patti for breakfast when she was in L.A. for some focus groups, and we hit it off immediately. She was new to the TV business, and I had exactly the right experience to help her. One of her biggest projects was to conduct consumer research on DISH's new on-screen program guide and remote control. This was one of my favorite projects at DirecTV; I had overseen all of the research for this and had personally conducted a lot of the usability testing. The partnership would be perfect for me and perfect for her. My only reservation was that DISH had earned a reputation for being thrifty, especially with consultants. Patti assured me things were changing in that area. We discussed the details of the project, I sent her a bid, she approved it, and in December 2013, I had my first consulting gig, and my new business was launched.

On the cancer front, my response to Crizotinib was going well, and I was handling the drug with minimal side effects. While the tumors had stopped shrinking, they were also not growing. And whether this was due to the chemo or the Crizotinib, it mattered not. Things were stable, and in the cancer world, stable is good. Dr. Ou saw no problem for me to travel, and he also told me that starting in 2014, we could now do CT scans every four months, instead of every two months.

Over the next few months, I went up to Denver for a week each month to conduct usability testing at DISH's headquarters in Englewood, Colorado. Their offices were beautiful, and the work went well. To counter the fatigue that came with Crizotinib, I loaded up on coffee and Mountain Dew, taking sips of each all day long. I knew I would crash when I came home and reverted back to my normal caffeine intake, but I wanted to be at my sharpest.

The only unpleasant part of these trips was the frigid weather. Even though most of my winter days in Colorado were bright and sunny, they were also bitter cold, with temperatures dipping down to as low as 7 degrees when I walked out of my hotel in the morning. It reminded me of my time in college in upstate New York. The cold was a prime reason why I moved to Los Angeles. But for the sake of a paycheck, I simply put on gloves and a warm coat and got through the chilly weather. It was a little strange to be doing work for DirecTV's biggest competitor. In the end, though, I concluded that we in the business world are the modern-day equivalent of mercenaries, selling our services to the highest bidder. Having been let go unceremoniously at DirecTV, it felt good to be appreciated once more. DISH was paying me well, and I was helping them build a better product. There is an old saying: don't get mad, get even.

Around the same time, I noticed that Herbalife was looking for a research director. I sent in my resume, but I heard nothing back. This was not unusual; companies receive so many resumes these days, it is hard for them to respond to each one. But in April, I noticed the job had been posted again, so I tried to find out who was the head of research at Herbalife and contact the person directly. I had searched all over LinkedIn but I couldn't find out who it was. I finally reached out to a friend, Sal Rodriguez, a former colleague at DirecTV who was now working at Herbalife, and asked if he could find the name for me. He got back to me in 10 minutes and told me her name was Emma. This was a good lesson in networking; Emma had not updated her LinkedIn profile, so there was no way I would have ever found her on my own. But because Sal worked there, he could find her easily.

Due to my age, I suspected it would be better to go back to a large company as a consultant, rather than as a full-time employee. I was also concerned that a new employer might find out about my cancer or my age and not hire me. As a consultant, there would be no need to go through human resources, and there would be no extensive background check. Consultants could be hired – and also let go – quickly, so this was a way to get around the corporate bureaucracy. I reached out to Emma by email, saying I knew she was looking for a director, but in the interim, I was available to step in immediately and help her with any research projects over the next few months. She emailed me back right away, and after a quick phone call, she invited me to come for an interview the next day. Herbalife had its global headquarters in downtown L.A., right next to L.A. Live and what was then Staples Center, where the Lakers and Kings played. The interview went well. Because Emma was very experienced in marketing research, she could quickly tell I was experienced, too. She invited me to start working there as a full-time consultant the following Monday. It all happened with astonishing quickness.

I had heard the rumors about Herbalife being a sketchy company, that some people accused it of running a pyramid scheme, and that its products were overpriced. They were also the subject of an investigation by the Federal Trade Commission. But years earlier, I became familiar with Amway, another company engaged in multi-level marketing, as a former girlfriend had been an Amway distributor. On the surface, both Amway and Herbalife struck me as companies that simply sold their products directly to consumers through distributors. More importantly though, after working in multinational corporations for more than three decades, I had no illusions about what business was really about – making money for the owners in whatever way possible. And for me, after 18 months of having doors slammed in my face for making the mistake of entering my mid-50s, my main concern was paying my bills and taking care of my family.

Having lost a job for contracting cancer, I was in no mood to judge a corporation on what someone else considered ethical issues. As it turned out, the federal investigation was instigated by an investor who had shorted Herbalife stock, meaning he had a vested interest in seeing the company fail and its stock price collapse. Whatever ethical lapses the company may or may not have participated in were no worse than what this two-faced investor was engaging in. It was yet another in a long list of lessons I had learned about the business world. Don't judge a book by its cover. That Herbalife was one of the few companies willing to take a chance on me spoke volumes about them. It also said a lot about the companies who passed me over.

I began working every day at Herbalife in April 2014. As I was a consultant who billed by the hour, I did not need to put in a 40-hour work week unless it was necessary. I worked as much as they wanted me to work. But unlike my past jobs with DirecTV and Disney Channel, I did not have a private office, and I would be in a cubicle. For me, that meant trouble.

The most obvious problem with working in a cubicle was that it put me in close physical proximity to others. Being sensitive to noise, that meant constant interruptions. There was one woman in particular whose voice had one volume setting – loud. I did my best to tune her out, but the more pressing issue that came with working in a shared space was in sharing germs. I typically caught a cold maybe once a year, but at Herbalife, I was suddenly catching a cold every two months. For someone with lung cancer, having difficulty breathing when I had a cold was hugely problematic.

Additionally, the fatigue was becoming a big issue. I did not want to be drinking caffeine all day long; this was okay at DISH, because it was just for a few days at a time. But at Herbalife, I was struggling with fatigue on a daily basis, and it was not fun. And then there was the additional problem of needing to take time off to go in for doctor visits and scans.

I did not tell Emma about my medical situation when I first interviewed with her, as I suspected that might torpedo any chances of getting work, even as a consultant. I did my best to hide it, but it all came to a head one warm day in June. I took the morning off to have my CT scans, which included the usual two hours of hydration at The Angeles Clinic. I neglected to tell Emma in advance. As fate would have it, she began emailing me that morning, seeking input for an afternoon meeting with a senior executive. I did my best to answer her questions, but I did not have my computer with me, so I was limited in how I could respond. And then when I entered the imaging center, I needed to turn my cell phone off entirely. After the scans were finished, I turned my phone back on and there were a dozen urgent texts and emails. I drove downtown and was dreading what would be awaiting me. As I walked into the office, a colleague told me that Emma wanted to see me immediately.

Once in Emma's office, she ordered me to close the door. The expression on her face was grim. She was not pleased with my being unavailable when she needed me. This type of expectation has become the norm in corporate America; there were some people at DirecTV who told me they set their alarm and woke up at 3:00 a.m. to check their phones, in case there were messages from their boss. While this was not the same situation, I could easily tell that I was in a lot of trouble.

"Where have you been?" she asked. "I can't have you disappear for hours at a time. This isn't working."

I nodded. Time to come clean.

"I had to go and have some medical tests," I said.

She stared and said nothing. I continued.

"I probably should have told you about my health situation upfront. I apologize."

I saw her looking at me more quizzically now. She motioned for me to continue.

"Two years ago," I said, "I was diagnosed with lung cancer. I've been through a number of treatments, and they've been successful. I'm currently on a clinical trial, and I'm taking a couple of pills each day, and the response has been great. I feel fine. But as part of the trial, I need to go in every four months and get tested. That's where I was today. Getting scans. Again, sorry for being tight-lipped, but not everyone is understanding about this sort of thing. In fact, at DirecTV, I was offered a severance package not long after I told my boss I had cancer. That's why I was reluctant to discuss it with you."

And with that, her expression softened. She went from tough, hard-driven executive to compassionate human being in an instant. She expressed sympathy, asked some questions about my medical situation, and we had a good chat. She told me she liked my work and wanted me to stay, and if I needed to take time off, that was fine, just give her some advance notice so she could plan ahead. All very reasonable. And then something unexpected happened.

That afternoon, I got a call from Dr. Lieber, who had just read the radiologist's report on my scans. He told me the results indicated there was progression of my cancer. He wanted me to come in the next day and meet with him.

18

Progression

Despite my initial success with Crizotinib, I never wanted to say I was in remission. Even though the tumor in my lung was now so small it was considered to be little more than scar tissue, I did not want to allow myself to think I was beating cancer. I felt that once I was diagnosed, I was in the club and it was a club for life. Not the type of club you'd want to join, but one you had to acknowledge. While the ROS1 cancer cells were inhibited from growing, they were likely still floating around in my body. It was admittedly a superstition, but I felt that if I ever implied that I was beating cancer, the disease would return. And when cancer returns, it is often harder to treat because it can develop resistance to further treatment.

The primary tumor had been identified in my lung, and the cancer had initially been thought to have spread to my pleural (chest) area, the lymph nodes, the kidney, and the liver. As we had only done a biopsy on the tumor in my lung, it was unclear whether the spots on my kidney and liver were actually tumors or just lesions. The scans I'd had over the years were merely highly detailed images, so we could not be fully certain if these were actually tumors. Lesions, unlike tumors, are simply damaged tissue, not necessarily cancerous. But all had shrunk during the chemo, and all had remained unchanged during the first 18 months on Crizotinib.

Over time, Dr. Lieber had speculated that some of these lesions might well have been benign cysts, which are even less of a concern. The only way to tell for certain is to have a biopsy, but with no growth, there was no reason to do so. For now, we would call them lesions, because we couldn't be quite sure of what they were, but we weren't about to say they were nothing. In June 2014 however, scans showed the lesions in my liver increased dramatically in size from the previous scans four months earlier. We had established I had two liver lesions, and both had grown substantially in this short span of time.

Dr. Lieber told me the lesions in my liver were still at a relatively small size, under 2 centimeters. That aspect was good. The possibility that they were growing rapidly was not good. It was also peculiar. I was experienced in the art of data analysis, having worked in marketing research for so long, and I was used to identifying trends. I kept a spreadsheet that monitored the size of each tumor (or lesion) that was mentioned in radiology reports. Building this spreadsheet may have stemmed from my obsessive nature, but it was also because I wanted to be an active participant in my cancer treatment. I would obviously never know as much about the science of cancer as my oncologists, but there were some things I did understand, and one of those things was math.

In my February 2014 scans, the lesions in my liver had decreased by 30 to 40 percent. We didn't question that, because why question good news? But it was very odd that these lesions would decrease in size and then do an about-face and dramatically increase just a few months later. My internet research told me I had none of the symptoms that typically affect patients with liver cancer. Something felt off.

The good news was that none of my other tumors or lesions had shown this yo-yo change in size. As I went back and re-read past radiology reports, I noticed that sometimes the radiologist did not even mention the size of a lesion, which often indicated it was too small to measure. A few reports just indicated there was no change at all. I spent some time speaking with my oncologist cousins, Paul and Steve, who told me that measurements of tumors and lesions were not always that accurate, as it was very difficult to pinpoint the exact size of these lesions. Different radiologists often measured using different techniques. I also noticed my scan reports tended to be written by a different radiologist each time. The whole situation was more than a little perplexing.

I went down to UC Irvine to consult with Dr. Ou. He assured me they would personally review these scans closely, as he didn't want me to have to leave the trial. But I also knew that if there really was progression in the tumors, I would likely have to go back onto chemo. I had been on Crizotinib for almost 2 years now, and I knew that it had stopped working on some patients. Dr. Ou told me there were a number of promising drugs in the pipeline for ROS1 patients like myself, and he expected to see a new clinical trial open for one of them in a few months. Like all clinical trials, nothing was guaranteed, and there was no way of knowing whether they'd be effective on me, for how long, or if I'd tolerate the side effects as well as I had tolerated those of Crizotinib.

My remarkable good luck with having doctors in the family continued. Cousin Paul's wife, Lisa, was a radiologist, and she agreed to take a look at the scans. I sent her the disks, and a few days later she got back to me with the answer. Unlike all of my previous CT scans, the scans done in February had been administered by the technician without IV contrast. This had made the tumors (or lesions) appear smaller than they actually were. When the June scans were done, IV contrast was used, and the tumors or lesions now appeared bigger. To only go back and draw comparisons with the most recent scan meant they had thought there was "growth," when, in fact, no growth at all was happening. Comparing the two scans was effectively comparing apples and oranges. This was likely just human error, either the technician had misinterpreted the oncologist's direction, or they simply made a mistake in not using contrast. I still wondered why the radiologist had not gone back and checked my previous scans beyond the most recent one, but apparently, that was not the protocol. The good news was that I could stay on the clinical trial, and continue using Crizotinib. Which led me to another issue.

When I first entered the trial, I had asked Dr. Ou about connecting with another patient who had been on the trial for a period of time. I wanted to speak with someone who was a little ahead of me in the journey and could help me know what to expect, to help light my path forward in a sense. My doctors were great, my cousins were generous with their time, but I also knew that doctors, family or not, were busy people, and I could only ask so much of them. I was finally feeling more comfortable in meeting others who were on Crizotinib, to compare notes, share experiences, and just have someone to talk to. I felt that only another stage 4 cancer patient would truly understand this situation.

After getting his approval, Dr. Ou put me in touch with Allen Fremont. As it turned out, Allen was not a typical cancer patient, nor a typical trial participant. Allen himself was a doctor who had graduated from Dartmouth Medical School, and he was not only extremely bright but a very nice guy as well. Allen was the second patient on the ROS1 clinical trial for Crizotinib. He had been diagnosed in 2011, one year before me, and had the wherewithal to seek out clinical trials on his own that might help him. He learned about the success doctors were having using Crizotinib to treat lung cancer patients whose tumors were identified as having the ALK mutation. Due to that success, Crizotinib was being expanded to try and treat a newly discovered genetic mutation, the ROS1 Rearrangement. He sought out the doctors working on it, and was lucky enough to test positive for ROS1.

Allen and I would meet periodically for breakfast at a local coffee shop. In addition to discussing hush-hush topics like our mortality, he provided some additional guidance that he had come across. As a physician, Allen was able to read up on and understand, a lot of the technical articles about the drug being tested in our trial. Crizotinib was effective at stopping the growth of the lung tumors, but Allen explained to me that it could not penetrate something called a blood-brain barrier. As a result, what sometimes happens to patients on Crizotinib is they develop brain tumors. He encouraged me to get a brain MRI every year, because the sooner any metastases to the brain were found, the more effectively they could be treated. I was lucky to have not been impacted by this, but I was able to pass this bit of information on to some other ROS1 patients who were unaware.

Allen and I were both very lucky to be treated by excellent doctors. In our experience visiting cancer internet sites, it was apparent that not all oncologists were as well-versed or as up-to-date on the most current treatments or techniques as ours were, especially those outside of the U.S. Allen and I stayed in touch for years, but the last time we met was when Andrea and I ran into him at UC Irvine before one of our appointments with Dr. Ou. He did not look good. He was optimistic, but optimism only goes so far. Allen passed away in early 2020, a jolting reminder that cancer can take even the most vigilant patient, one who was keenly aware of what was happening and did all the right things to fight the disease. As I moved forward in my own journey, I couldn't help but notice the numerous patients I had met who ultimately fell victim to a recurrence of their cancer.

There is, naturally, an inherent sadness to being afflicted with this disease. People would post online that they had decided to stop treatment, or had entered hospice, as they did not want to endure any more pain. I noticed these were coming more from patients who had worked in the medical field, possibly because they had seen the ravages of the disease, and wanted to end things before the cancer made staying alive more difficult than it already was. Their deaths often came sooner than any of us expected.

Left untreated, cancer can move quickly through the body. The ROS1 Rearrangement cells were particularly aggressive, and especially dangerous because it often led to rapid and uncontrolled growth of the cancer. There have even been indications it can be effective on patients who have other types of ROS1-related cancers, ones that go beyond lung cancer. But

Crizotinib cannot kill all the cancerous cells in the body. Over time, these cancerous cells can acquire resistance to Crizotinib, and the drug may stop working. The cancer returns, and while a different drug can sometimes be effectively employed at that point, not everyone responds well.

Around this time, I became acquainted with the ROS1ders, a Facebook group started by three patients who had ROS1-positive lung cancer. One of the co-founders, a lung cancer survivor named Janet Freeman-Daily, started taking Crizotinib around the same time I did, and she experienced a similar level of success. Janet, an MIT-trained engineer, became a patient advocate who immersed herself in the subject of lung cancer after she was diagnosed in 2011.

The ROS1ders became more than just an advocacy group that served as a resource for both ROS1 patients and health care providers. In addition to providing accurate medical information and sharing patient experiences, the ROS1ders actively collaborate with cancer researchers and other nonprofits to accelerate research. They are working with a group at the University of Colorado to generate ROS1+ cancer models that will move research forward. It is a great example of patients not just networking, but actively working to accelerate the development of new treatments for cancer.

19

High School

It goes without saying that having cancer changes the way you look at the world. It changes how you go about living your life, and how you plan for the future, because the future becomes uncertain. You don't know what your longevity will be, and you don't know what your finances will look like. Cancer treatments, like health insurance, can be expensive. You don't know if they will work, and if they do, you don't know how long they'll work, or what side effects they'll bring with them. But life still goes on around you. Your life may be in flux, but other people's lives are moving firmly ahead.

Around the time I started on the Crizotinib trial, Matthew was entering 8th grade, and we began looking around at high schools. We were living within the boundaries of the Los Angeles Unified School District, which was far from ideal. Our local high school was Venice High, and we were becoming increasingly uneasy about enrolling Matthew there. Gang-related shootings had been reported on their campus, and a tour of the school did little to make us comfortable. As we considered alternatives, I started to nervously reflect upon my own experiences attending a gritty inner-city high school in New York. The education I received there went beyond academics.

DeWitt Clinton High School was once a well-regarded school in the Bronx, and its graduates included author James Baldwin, fashion designer Ralph Lauren, actor Burt Lancaster, and playwright Neil Simon. Stan Lee, the driving force behind Marvel Comics, also went there. But they attended Clinton decades before I did, and it was now better known for producing basketball players than creative geniuses. It was a huge, all-boys school of more than 4,000 students. The absence of girls, coupled with simmering racial tension that was particularly ripe in the 1970s, made for a very unpleasant experience.

I was fortunately placed in an honors program of 90 boys called the scholarship class, and we received a more rigorous academic curriculum. The teachers were good. But high school for me was something to get through, rather than an enriching experience. In an incident that happened during my first month there, three guys jumped me in a back staircase. One brandished a knife, and while I only lost some pocket change, the experience left me shaken. I learned what to do and what not to do. I rarely used the bathroom in school, and I frequently ate lunch in the library. I came and left school each day with friends. My high school experience was good at teaching me how to deal with adversity, but it was not exactly how your formative years were supposed to be. I wanted Matthew to have something better.

We began exploring private high schools in our area, but we soon learned they were very competitive to get into. Many were K-12, enrolling kids in kindergarten, and keeping them straight through to 12th grade. The openings they had for high school were limited. We applied to two schools on the Westside and three schools in the San Fernando Valley. The schools in the Valley would be a little easier to get accepted into, but there would be a 30 to 45-minute commute each way. The fact that I didn't have a full-time job made me uneasy about the tuition, which was far from cheap. But in going through my cancer experience, I had started to become more comfortable walking through the fog of uncertainty. We'd figure out some way to pay for it.

Part of my job search involved setting up networking meetings with a variety of consultants in the marketing research business. One very prescient meeting I arranged was with Glen Friedman, who had worked for DirecTV years earlier. We chatted for about 30 minutes in his Century City office, and he gave me a few job search leads. We talked about collaborating on an upcoming project he had. I mentioned near the end of our talk, more anecdotally than for any other reason, that Matthew would be applying to the Windward School, where both of Glen's sons were attending. As I left his office and walked to the elevator, he came out and gave me what turned out to be the best advice possible when it came to applying to this school.

"Be sure to tell them that you're living in the same neighborhood," he said. "It will absolutely make a big difference."

As it turned out, he was absolutely correct. Private schools like to stay on good terms with their neighbors, and that tidbit of advice was key in getting Matthew accepted to Windward, which was six blocks from our house. He was also accepted to two of the schools in the Valley, but when you can walk to classes, it beats a long commute. And ironically, getting let go from DirecTV had an unforeseen benefit. When we applied to these private schools, I listed my occupation as the president of Chill Research. Owning your own business carries more weight than being a director in a large corporation. Private schools themselves are businesses, and they rely on donations to build new classrooms and upgrade facilities, so they focus on parents who have the means to help in their fundraising. Little did they know I was making a good bit less money than I had been at DirecTV. Perception is everything.

Windward turned out to be a great place for Matthew, and he blossomed there. He developed a lot of great friendships, and the small class sizes allowed for individual attention. He made the basketball and volleyball teams, and I got to see him play in a lot of his games. This was yet another advantage I had by not working at a demanding corporate job. I didn't know how much time I had left, but I was fortunate to be able to devote some of it to the truly important things in life. When I was working at Disney and DirecTV, flying around the country, and spending my days in endless meetings, I missed some parts of Matthew growing up. It's the price that parents often pay to fund a certain lifestyle. It is a conundrum. We need to make money to pay for nice things, but with that comes a cost.

Having grown up in a not-so-great environment, I wanted to give my son some of the opportunities I didn't have. But just as importantly, I wanted him to be safe, and for him to know he was safe. Unlike at the high school I attended, the danger factor at Windward was largely eliminated. One less thing to worry about, which was good. There were plenty of other worries popping up for me.

20

Ongoing Medical Issues

My consulting gig with Herbalife had been going well, so I asked Emma if I could work from home and she agreed. I'm an early riser, so I would often start work at 5:00 a.m., put in 4 hours, and then be ready for a break when most everyone else was just starting their day. Designing and running research surveys was something I typically did alone, and could do it at any hour. Unlike my days at DirecTV, I didn't need to attend a lot of meetings. I was no longer on the fast track, and I was no longer missing it. I felt as if I was inching back into a life of normalcy, and a life with a future.

The Crizotinib was keeping the cancer at bay. The tumors were no longer shrinking, but neither were they growing, and there were some days when I would rarely think about my illness or my longevity. I felt closer and closer to becoming my old self. I was developing a comfortable routine, although admittedly the routine also included going in once a month to get stuck with a needle in order to have a blood test. Normal can be whatever you define it to be.

My CT scans showed no change in the size of the tumor in my lung, and that was when the radiologists even bothered to mention it in their reports. A part of me wondered if the cancer would one day vanish, and I could stop taking Crizotinib. I learned, however, that cancer likely returns if the patient stops treatment. My case might have been a little different since I had been on the drug for so long – but neither Dr. Lieber nor Dr. Ou thought it was at all worth the risk of stopping. I had been tolerating the drug very well. I had essentially become one of the many people for whom cancer was becoming little more than a chronic condition, rather than a death sentence. Andrea and Matthew were getting comfortable with the possibility that I'd be around for years as well.

I continued to write books, and I was publishing two mystery novels regularly every year. I met friends for lunch. Andrea and I had date nights and went to movies and concerts. We took Matthew to Laker games and USC football games. We went on vacations. As Matthew neared the end of high school, we went with him to visit colleges throughout California, and then took an east coast swing.

Even though I had gone to USC for graduate school, I did not push Matthew to go there. Since I'd written a series of books about a fictional former USC football player-turned-private investigator, Matthew knew how invested I was with the school. I wanted him to go somewhere that he could claim as his. The fact that tuition at USC had soared to $50,000 a year then, 10 times what it was when I attended, maybe played a role in that line of thinking. But I told him he could go where he wanted to go. I didn't want to limit him, the way my father had been forced to limit me. Matthew was a straight-A student, so he was accepted at most of the schools he applied to. In the end, it came down to USC, UCLA, and UC Berkeley. He chose Berkeley, which is a great school. It was relatively affordable. He'd get to live away from home, but he'd be close enough to drive to in one day. And after we took him up there for the start of freshman year, we became empty nesters. We missed him a lot, but we were ending up where we should be at this stage of life. We were back on track.

It's not that health problems didn't spring up. One set of CT scans went terribly wrong when the technician tried to hook me up with the IV tube to add contrast and missed the vein. The contrast went straight into my left arm, and the pain was excruciating. I yelled at her and demanded she pull the IV out of my arm. Someone else came in and hooked it up correctly in my right arm, but after the scan, my left forearm puffed up freakishly and approached the size of a football. In a frantic conversation with Cousin Paul, I asked if I should go to the ER, but he calmed me down and said these things occur more often than I would imagine, and that the swelling should go down the next day. It did, but when this first happens to you, it is terrifying.

Another scary moment occurred, one that indeed had life-or-death consequences. I was in The Angeles Clinic one warm, summer morning, getting hydration prior to my CT scans. I was wearing cargo shorts and a t-shirt, standard gear for me when I needed something comfortable to be sitting around in all day. The traveling nurse who was monitoring my IV drip happened to notice my calves were swollen. I shrugged and told her that had been the case for years, and was very likely due to taking the Crizotinib. Nevertheless, she pointed it out to Dr. Lieber, who examined me for a moment, and then said he'd set up an ultrasound for right after the hydration.

"Can I do this after lunch?" I asked, knowing I hadn't eaten anything all day in preparation for the scans.

"I think you should go to lunch later," he replied.

When a doctor indicates that delaying things an extra hour might have consequences, you pay attention. I walked over to St. John's Medical Center and spent an hour there getting tested, and then the technician directed me back to Dr. Lieber's office, where I received some unpleasant news. I had a small blood clot in one of my legs. When caught early, it can be adequately dealt with; without treatment, the blood clot could dislodge and move through the bloodstream with dire results. Untreated, this could prove fatal in a matter of months.

Dr. Lieber put me on a drug called Eliquis, a pill taken twice a day. I never had any symptoms, in part because the blood clot was still fairly small. Had I not been wearing shorts, and had I not run into that particular traveling nurse, who only stayed at The Angeles Clinic for a few months, it was entirely possible my good health would have been placed in serious jeopardy. Finding and treating a serious condition quickly was imperative. I had been extraordinarily lucky when the tumor in my lung was found while it was still relatively small. Now, once more, identifying this blood clot right away prevented a nasty outcome. Somehow I was dodging bullets.

A few months after all that, I went in to see my dermatologist of many years about a rash on my side. We had just gotten back from Hawaii, and the many red splotches on my skin made me wonder if the hotel had bed bugs. No, he told me, glancing at the skin. I had a mild case of shingles. This is why I liked going to this elderly dermatologist, he had seen it all and recognized things quickly. He noticed a different red mark on my arm and told me we should test it. I said sure, but before I could say anything else, he had his special glasses on and was numbing my arm up, and starting to do a biopsy. He was also well into his 80s and I held my breath that his hands would be steady, which they were. The doctor's hunch was correct, I had the beginnings of a skin cancer called basal cell carcinoma, unrelated to the lung cancer.

Soon after that appointment and diagnosis, I reluctantly switched doctors, choosing to have a younger dermatologist remove the skin cancer. I realized I may have been practicing ageism myself, but there does come a point where concerns over physical well-being can take precedence over trying to remain unbiased.

West Los Angeles is comprised of an aging population, which is quite different from how it was when I first moved to southern California. Back in the late 1970s, areas like Westwood, Santa Monica, Venice, and Marina del Rey were all hip spots to live and play. They were full of bars, clubs, movie theaters and music venues, and I spent many a weekend night there. But it's as if the youngsters who moved there back then had put down roots and never left. The same young hipsters from 40 or 50 years ago were now aging hipsters, either collecting Social Security or close to it. Our doctors, once bright and youthful, were still bright, but no longer so youthful.

At one point, I needed hernia surgery. But the leading doctors in the area were all in their 70s. The surgeon I finally settled on was 74, but still spry, and getting good reviews on Yelp, hardly the type of bullet-proof confirmation I would have liked. The other new trend I was encountering was that some primary care physicians were starting concierge practices, which meant patients needed to fork over thousands of dollars upfront every year, to just get in the door.

In concierge medicine, patients receive lengthy appointments with their doctors. They have plenty of time to ask a myriad of questions, and perhaps most importantly, to be given thorough and detailed explanations of their maladies. The bad part is the prohibitive cost. One reason for this shift was due to doctors' frustrations over having to spend too much of their day on bureaucratic matters, like securing insurance approval for procedures. But it was also due to the huge jump in L.A. real estate prices over the years, especially on the Westside.

This meant more patients could afford concierge medicine, but it also meant that fewer young doctors could afford to buy a home in the area – so they often chose to open practices elsewhere. So our area had quite a lot of older physicians practicing – some of whom were unavailable to me, which created a problem of sorts. Many patients were choosing to pay the high cost of having a concierge doctor. I just wasn't one of them.

21

The End Of The Trial

At the end of Matthew's senior year in high school, a friend of his was given a graduation gift of a trip to Europe with his parents. He was told he could bring a few friends along, and Matthew was invited. The trip would start in Rome, go up through Venice, and end in London. Andrea and I decided to escort Matthew to Rome and pick him up in London. We did get to spend a little time with the host family at the beginning and end of the boys' trip, but for the most part, we did our own thing, skipping Venice and going to Scotland instead, then taking a train down to London. We had a great time, and we began to think of foreign trips to do on our own. We were approaching the age when this was supposed to happen.

The following year, Andrea and I went to Croatia and Slovenia. It was a nice trip, but it did not end well. We planned to spend the last two nights in Venice, Italy, but upon arrival, we had to pass through Venice airport. While getting off of an automated people mover, I saw the end of it was blocked by a group of people standing and talking. I tried to navigate past them while steering my suitcase. No such luck. I tripped and fell, and I knew I had a big problem before I even hit the ground. My left leg was in severe pain.

The airport personnel came by to help, and they wheeled me to an emergency room on the lower concourse. Yes, some airports have ERs. The doctor on duty told me I had probably pulled a hamstring. He injected me with a painkiller, but he advised me that it would only help temporarily. He wrote a prescription, likely for an opioid, but it was in Italian, so I couldn't be certain. Andrea went off to get it filled at a local pharmacy, but I knew there was no way I could make it onto the water taxi we were supposed to catch, nor up any stairs that might be at our hotel. We rearranged our itinerary to fly home the next morning, but we had to spend the night sleeping on benches in Venice airport. Every hour, a different pair of Italian soldiers dressed in fatigues came by on patrol, carrying long guns, often asking what we were doing there. We told them that was a good question. As you might imagine, we got very little sleep that night.

The one advantage to air travel when you're injured is the use of a wheelchair. I was barely able to navigate the 10 steps from our bench to the men's room, so a wheelchair was our only option to reach the gate. It turned out to be amazing. For us, the long lines to move through airport security in Venice were bypassed. We were practically waived right through.

We had to change planes in Amsterdam, and a tight 45-minute connection was easy with someone wheeling me along. I placed our carry-on bags in my lap as we sailed through the terminal to board our connecting flight home. The trip was a breeze. That I was sky-high on painkillers made this a remarkably pleasant 12-hour flight. Even when we arrived in L.A., getting through customs took about 10 minutes instead of the normal 60-plus. The problems, of course, really began when we finally got home, and I sobered up enough to seek out some good old-fashioned American medical treatment. I did not get what I expected.

Having cancer taught me to be very selective in picking doctors. The extent of my leg injury was such that I wanted to see an orthopedist right away. So I did what one does in a time of urgency; I picked one with good ratings on the internet. The one I found was in a large orthopedic group on the Westside, which allowed patients to simply walk in if they needed care right away.

After being examined by the initial doctor, she referred me to the one who specialized in injuries to the legs. My experience with him was about as bad as you could imagine. This orthopedist ordered an MRI with contrast. I told him that because of my high creatinine levels from being on Crizotinib, my kidneys were not in ideal shape and that I'd need to do hydration prior to the MRI. The orthopedist gave me a blank look and said, incorrectly, if I needed hydration, maybe I should just drink a bottle of Gatorade. When I asked him if he could recommend a physical therapist, he raved about one in particular, only to say the PT wasn't taking on new patients. This doctor also suspected I might have a back problem, and he said if the pain got too intense, he could have his "injection guy" give me a shot to the spine. At this point, my biggest goal was to get out of his office as quickly as possible.

The MRI revealed a partial tear in my right hamstring, and the best healing method was time and physical therapy. I checked with my insurance company and found a clinic near my house. My physical therapist turned out to be a part-time actor, and after one session of watching him spend more time on his phone than working with me, I decided to move on. A friend recommended a physical therapist in Brentwood, and she was very good. Unfortunately, she was headed out for a two-week vacation, and her associate who treated me next clearly did not know what she was doing. After one session, my leg felt worse than it had since the accident.

Finally, Andrea's uncle Bob mentioned he was seeing an excellent person, who was more of a trainer than a licensed physical therapist, but he was very good. His studio was in a converted garage behind his house, and he only accepted cash or Venmo. As it turned out, he was fantastic, and just what I needed. His background was as an athlete and a dancer, which ordinarily would have given me pause. But after bad experiences with both licensed PTs and with an orthopedist who had not bothered to keep up with modern medicine for a few decades, I was ready to try alternatives.

My recovery hit a snag a month later, though. I felt well enough to roast a turkey on Thanksgiving, but after taking the bird out of the oven for basting, I felt a sharp pain in my leg. *In my other leg.* I had been making so much of an effort to not put too much strain on my healing left leg, that I ended up putting too much on the right leg. It took a good eight months of therapy and regular exercises before both legs returned to being close to normal.

Near the end of 2018, the clinical trial at UC Irvine ended. Crizotinib had been approved by the FDA for ROS1 patients, and the trial had run its course like all trials eventually do. Dr. Ou arranged for me to begin getting Crizotinib through CVS Specialty, which was a division of CVS that focused on medications for rare conditions. There was a $200 per month co-pay, that Pfizer kindly waived. While it was nice that I would no longer need to drive down to Orange County every two months to get the drug, that turned out to be a double-edged sword; I would now need to make sure I was at home when the delivery person arrived.

Crizotinib comes with a retail price tag of more than $20,000 per month, although most people don't pay anywhere near that. With a drug that expensive, I practically expected it to come in an armored car. Instead, it was brought by a delivery company, whose drivers arrived in unmarked cars and did not bother to knock or ring the doorbell. My desk faced the front yard, so I had an unobstructed view of their protocol. The driver would walk up to the front door, place the wildly expensive one-month supply of Crizotinib on the welcome mat, take a photo of it, and drive off. That's it. No email notification, no text, no bell ringing, no nothing. I had $20,000 worth of drugs sitting unattended on my porch.

Calls to CVS Specialty only resulted in their placing a note in my file, instructing the driver to knock on the front door, which they rarely did. If we worked outside the home, this would have been hugely problematic. I was glad I could wait at home for the delivery but sighed at having to make sure either myself or Andrea were eyeing the front of the house all day, ready to grab the drug before any porch pirate could get their hands on it.

In the end, these were minor inconveniences, especially when compared with other challenges in my life. These were manageable. This was what I had wanted, the ability to keep going through the day-to-day challenges of life that everyone faces. This was real. This was a normal life. Or as normal as I could expect life to be.

22

Spirituality

There is a belief that when a loved one is being operated on, the waiting room holds no atheists. We can't be certain there is a God, but we can be certain that saying a few prayers never hurt. And even though my life now was now returning to a nice routine, I had become more spiritual, in the way many people become more spiritual when faced with crises that seem above and beyond what they can endure. My beliefs were beginning to evolve.

I had never been an especially religious person. When I was in my 20s and 30s, in fact, I liked to refer to myself an agnostic. It wasn't that I didn't believe in God, it was more like I didn't think it mattered. But that was then. Things change.

In 2008, as Andrea and I were mired in an ever-deepening financial woe, I found myself sinking deeper and deeper into a depression. I can vividly recall a moment when I was staring out of my office window one rainy afternoon. The door to my office was closed. I looked at the stormy weather, and I felt the darkness of the day echoing into my soul. At that point, I had been getting two or three hours of sleep a night and was feeling as if the walls were closing in. I was becoming weak and fearful, and everything I disliked in a person. And as I gazed out my office window into the gloomy day, I arrived at a moment when, staring up at the black clouds and listening to rain pelt the windows, I softly uttered a few choice words, almost involuntarily.

"Please help me."

I'm not sure how I came to say that, to ask for help, because as someone who was not religious, I did not pray. I did not go to any religious services, and I thought the Bible was a collection of wonderful stories written by someone with a very clever imagination.

My religious background as a child was frustrating, much like my relationship with my father. My parents were Jewish, so I was Jewish, although we did not go to services regularly. Between the ages of 8 and 13, I was required to attend Hebrew school in the afternoons, following the end of my regular school classes. Or I was supposed to.

The first year of Hebrew school was very interesting. We read the great stories in the Bible: Adam and Eve, Noah and the Ark, King Solomon and the baby. They were interesting, and at 8 years old I was in no position to question whether or not these events actually happened. I just assumed they did. I liked learning about them.

But then, from my second year on, our studies were devoted to learning how to read and write Hebrew, always delving into prayer books. That's it. No more interesting stories, just a lot of drudgery, reading prayers I did not understand, in a language no one I knew spoke. By the end of my second year, I had largely stopped attending. Instead, I would go off and play sports with my friends. My parents were never informed about my absences, and I'm not sure the Hebrew school even noticed.

My father was observant to a point, although he himself did not attend services regularly; his job with the post office often required him to work on Saturdays, when services were held. He insisted we keep kosher inside our home, but we could eat whatever we wanted outside. None of that made any sense to me. And from my first ham sandwich at the fabled Automat in Manhattan, I became a lover of all food, the more exotic, the better. My mother would occasionally smuggle shrimp or lobster into the house when my father wasn't there, but we were careful to remove the shells before he returned.

My break from Judaism happened just before I turned 13 and had my bar mitzvah. It was October 1969, and there was a tight mayoral race in New York City. I had become interested in politics for the same reason I had become interested in sports and movies: it was very entertaining. There were three candidates running for mayor that year, and all three were going to speak, separately, at a local event, held at our temple. I think they chose our temple because it was large and could host a lot of people.

I went to the political event with my father, and I was excited about it. But a strange thing happened when we arrived. As we walked into the temple, my father insisted I cover my head because we were in the "House of God." In most cases, this would have meant wearing a hat or a yarmulke, but we did not have one for me. So, my father unfolded his handkerchief and insisted I wear it on top of my head to honor God.

My father refused to negotiate on this, and I don't think I've ever felt so humiliated, nor have I ever really forgiven him for making me endure this. People pointed at me and laughed. As far as Judaism was concerned, this was the last straw for me. I never denied my background, but from then on, I saw being Jewish as a cultural identity, not a religious one. I liked the food and I liked some of the holidays. I liked Jewish people, and as I grew older, I found I had a better connection with Jewish girls. But that would be the extent of my involvement with organized religion going forward. Aside from attending a few required bar mitzvahs and weddings over time, I did not set foot in another temple for services ever again.

Jumping ahead almost forty years later, I found myself suddenly staring out into a dark day, and asking God to help me. I didn't really know how to pray, and the idea of asking God to send me buyers for our house, ones who also had a large down payment ready sounded more than a little inappropriate. Instead, I prayed for strength, prayed for this mess to be over, and asked for forgiveness for all sins I may or may not have ever committed. I did not notice any major changes in the coming months, and at times I wondered if God was trying to figure out who I was.

I briefly thought of attending services again, but realistically, it had never felt very good to me. It had never brought me any peace, and saying prayers in a language I didn't understand never gave me any comfort. But I did stumble across something else. As was my custom, being an early riser, I woke early one Sunday morning and turned on the TV. I'm not sure of the last channel we happened to be watching the night before, but up popped Joel Osteen, preaching his mantra of putting your faith in God, and he'll take you to places you never dreamed you could go. I was suddenly willing to listen.

I had heard of Joel Osteen, but I didn't know much about him. I had previously assumed he was like most of the other fire-and-brimstone-style Christian preachers that came on TV every Sunday morning. I had seen a few of these before, and I didn't really pay attention to their admonitions that I would be going straight to hell if I didn't follow their guidance. But there was something about what Joel Osteen said that morning that resonated with me, and I began watching his show regularly. Even when we got past our financial woes, I still watched, simply because I thought it was interesting. I found myself praying more and worrying less. It was helping.

When I was diagnosed with cancer, Joel Osteen's show became an important part of my Sunday routine, right up there with setting aside time for watching NFL football. I did not buy a Bible, but I did read some of Osteen's books. I did not join his church, but I did send him a small donation, just like I send donations to my high school alumni association and to organizations working on cancer research. At the time, I was unaware of how polarizing his ministry was, but for me, it mattered not. His talks helped me get through a rough patch in my life. I doubt my donations added much to their coffers; doing so simply made me feel good. You take your inspiration where you can find it.

I still did not have much faith in organized religion. I'd seen too many stories of corruption and was not about to go all in. But I began to believe I could have a one-on-one relationship with God. And as our financial crisis ended, I hoped my cancer crisis would end, too. Being an agnostic was fine when things were going well. When the tide turned, it no longer felt so good. Time to change course.

The one problem I could never reconcile, though, was that there were so many good people who had had their lives shortened by cancer. There were certainly people who had been far more religious than I was, who had undoubtedly been praying their whole lives.

Maybe they had lived better lives. Why did these people not have their prayers answered? Why was I blessed with such good luck?

The answer is unknown, of course, but I presumed it might be that God has a plan for all of us. And while we could make our own choices, God could steer us in whatever direction he wanted. It still didn't help me understand why an innocent child would die of cancer, while a grumpy old man might live for decades with the disease. Some answers remain shrouded in mystery. But soon, an even bigger mystery was forming in the world. A dark cloud that would come to overshadow everything else. And again, there would be no good explanation for it.

23

Living Through Covid

In 2020, the global pandemic eclipsed everything in our lives. I skipped my scheduled CT scans in April, as positive Covid-19 tests mounted, and reports of overburdened hospitals ran wild. Watching healthcare workers covered head-to-toe in protective gear made me think I didn't want to be anywhere near a hospital, an imaging center, or even a doctor's office. There were a lot of unanswered questions about Covid, no vaccines were yet available, and reports of death tolls kept climbing. For someone with lung cancer, the idea of having my breathing impacted and potentially needing a respirator if I caught the virus kept us socially isolated for a long time.

There were, however, a few additional challenges for us in 2020. Matthew was in Australia, for the spring semester of his junior year in college. He was at the University of New South Wales, in Sydney. We had been planning to visit him in April, but with Covid raging, we began to re-think our trip. Matthew's girlfriend, Jen, was about to go see him over spring break in mid-March. She'd gone to the airport and was waiting to board her plane. Matthew then learned that Australia had just implemented a strict lockdown plan, and anyone entering Australia would have to quarantine for two weeks. Those not following this rule would be subject to harsh penalties, up to and including going to jail.

Matthew quickly called Jen, and she was able to cancel her trip and get her luggage off the plane. At that point, we asked Matthew about the wisdom of him staying any longer in Australia, especially since his classes would all be remote. He could take them as easily from his bedroom in Los Angeles as from his dorm room in Sydney. He agreed, and said he could be packed in an hour if we could get him onto a flight.

Interestingly, getting the flight was the easiest part of his return. Not only were there plenty of open seats, but the prices had fallen dramatically. Whereas his flight going to Sydney cost well over a thousand dollars, the flight coming home cost only a few hundred. If you didn't mind the risk of possibly being hooked up to a ventilator afterward, this was a wonderful way to travel on the cheap, and much less crowded. Matthew arrived back in L.A. on March 17th, and we celebrated St. Patrick's Day at home, albeit Andrea and I in our living room, and Matthew quarantined in his bedroom.

The bigger issue we had, though, was trying to get Matthew health insurance here. Since he was planning to be in Australia for the first five months of the year, we cancelled his health insurance policy in the U.S. and arranged for a different policy in Australia. When we tried to get him back onto our health plan, we were told he could not begin coverage until the first day of the following month, which was April 1.

Two weeks without health insurance is usually a safe bet for a healthy 21-year-old. But being on the overly cautious side, with a strong respect for Murphy's Law, that whatever could go wrong would go wrong, we began looking into temporary health insurance. From slip-and-fall injuries to a possible car accident, there were a host of possibilities once you let your imagination run amok. What I learned, though, was that getting legitimate, temporary health insurance in California without a brief waiting period was virtually impossible, no matter what we were willing to pay.

A few years earlier, many health insurance companies offered a type of temporary health coverage. This was designed for people traveling in California, ones who may have had health insurance elsewhere, but under policies that did not cover out-of-state or out-of-country medical expenses. As the cost of health care skyrocketed however, some people could no longer afford traditional health insurance and were periodically using these temporary travel-based health plans. California eventually eliminated this kind of coverage, declaring it inadequate, saying it did not meet the minimum state requirements. But insurance companies still maintained the practice of requiring "new" enrollees to wait until the first day of the following month for coverage to take effect. There would be a gap for anyone like Matthew, who needed immediate health insurance and couldn't have planned for it ahead of time. We also explored getting Medi-Cal for him, but we learned we would not qualify for it.

After an exhaustive search, we thought we had found a possible solution, which turned out to be a faith-based health plan. The price was reasonable but the details were sketchy, and we were having trouble understanding the specifics of what was covered under the plan. We asked Andrea's uncle Bob, an attorney, if he would read the fine print and explain it to us. He read it and told us this health care plan was not required to compensate us for any health care expense Matthew might incur. The insurance company would decide what they would or would not cover, and this would be done after the fact. It was technically not health insurance, but rather, a "medical cost sharing plan." The only thing they committed to was that they would pray very hard for all of their members.

While prayers were nice, they could not be a stand-in for traditional healthcare coverage. So, we simply asked Matthew to stay in his room for two weeks and self-quarantine, which was what the CDC guidelines advised for anyone coming into the country, anyway. Matthew's girlfriend, Jen, came over and visited a lot, which kept him happy to be semi-isolated for a couple of weeks. But over the course of the year, another cancer-related issue arose that would affect all of our lives.

Jen's mother had been diagnosed with breast cancer a couple of years earlier. She had gone through the standard regimen of chemo, radiation, and surgery, and her oncologist believed she was in full remission. Matthew introduced me to Jen's mom the year before, as she and a friend were planning to write a book about their experience, along the lines of *The Girlfriends' Guide To Getting Through Cancer.* I shared my experiences of writing and publishing books with her, and we talked about our cancer journeys. Interestingly, Jen's mom was also named Andrea, and she was also a psychologist, working as a professor at Occidental College. Everything seemed to be going well for her. Until it wasn't. Her breast cancer returned in 2020, and it returned with a vengeance.

It was in May that Jen's mom learned her cancer had come back, shortly after Matthew had returned from Australia. Despite treatment, she passed away just six months later. It was a grim reminder of how quickly cancer can move, and how devastating it can be. There are few things as hard as losing your mother, but it was exceptionally tough to have it happen to a 21-year-old. The pandemic had prompted Jen to move back down from Berkeley to southern California, and she had been living with her mother in their apartment in Pasadena. The unit was pricey, and as a student, it would be a stretch for Jen to live there by herself and pay a high rent. So, not only was she losing her mother, she was losing her home as well.

Jen moved in with us in November 2020 and stayed until she and Matthew graduated the following May. With many businesses and entertainment places closed during this period, we were all cocooning. Our big event of the day was dinner, and Andrea went overboard to make each evening meal special. When Matthew had initially left for college, the empty nest syndrome hit us hard, not just because of his absence, but because we sensed he would likely only come home for short periods: school breaks and summer vacations. Everything about this period of time during the pandemic was unexpected and challenging, but we ended up relishing having the two of them with us.

And as upending as life during the pandemic was, more changes were headed our way, ones that would have ramifications for my own healthcare situation. We would soon learn that a nodule had formed in my lung during 2019, a surreptitious land mine that had gone undetected for two full years. A nodule is considered to be a lesion that is less than 3 centimeters. It was small but it was worrisome. This was not good.

24

A New Cancer Emerges

The impact of the pandemic spread far and wide, and it affected the cancer world. My cancer world. After a year of working from home, Dr. Lieber, the oncologist who steered me through 9 years of cancer treatments, had decided to retire. He was in his late 60s and told me he wanted to do other things in his life, like spending time with his family, hiking, and perhaps most important, having a normal sleep pattern. He would sometimes call me with scan results well into the evening, so I knew he worked a lot of long hours and kept a grueling schedule. I hated to lose him, but I knew he deserved a retirement. I told him I could never thank him enough for everything he had done for me.

Dr. Lieber suggested I begin seeing a lung cancer specialist who was at The Angeles Clinic, but I liked the idea of seeing a generalist, one who would reach out to specialists when needed. I'd seen another oncologist a few times when Dr. Lieber had been away, and I appreciated his knowledge and experience. Dr. Formal had been practicing for many years, and like Dr. Lieber, he saw patients with many different types of cancers. Looking back on it, I'm not sure what I wanted was a generalist. What I really wanted was another Dr. Lieber. That was not what I got.

I think it's safe to say that choosing the right oncologist is one of the most important decisions a cancer patient will ever make. It is not unlike entering a relationship. The majority of your joy and misery for many years can emanate from that one crucial move. Dr. Lieber had a quick mind; I would ask a question, he would give an answer, and we'd move forward. I liked that. If I needed more detail, he'd provide it. My 9 years with him had been extraordinary; we had overcome the dour expectations of my initial prognosis. I could not have asked for a better doctor.

But sadly, Dr. Formal did not work in the same way. Each question I asked was given a long, thorough answer, and while it was comprehensive, I already knew half of what he was telling me. I waited patiently for him to finish before I could slip in my next question. What could have been a 10-minute conversation would sometimes drag on to 45 minutes. But all of that could have been endured, because in the end, smart doctors typically make smart decisions, and that's what you want, especially in an oncologist.

With the pandemic making me uneasy about entering any medical facility unless it was absolutely necessary, I only did CT scans once during 2020. In May 2021, I went in for a new round of scans, and Dr.

Formal's assistant called afterward to schedule an appointment for the next day. This did not sound promising. When doctors want you to come into the office, there's usually a good reason, and the reason itself is rarely good.

"It appears there's a new nodule in your lung," he began. "It's small, only 7 millimeters, but it's been growing in size."

"Are you certain of this?" I asked cautiously. I had been tracking my scans carefully, and this was the first I had heard of any real progression in the disease. I knew that different radiologists measured things differently. When a nodule was this small – and 7 millimeters was tinier than the size of a pencil eraser – it was tough to get an accurate read.

"Yes," he assured me, and he told me the same radiologist had gone back to my 2020 scans and measured this nodule at 5 millimeters, and also looked back to 2019 when it was 3 millimeters. Nothing had been mentioned in any of my previous scan reports, so I was taken aback. The radiologist who wrote the earlier reports either did not notice these things or did not think that they were worth mentioning.

"So, the good news is that it's growing slowly," I said. "The bad news is it's growing at all."

Dr. Formal confirmed this was indeed the case. They did not know if this nodule had the ROS1 Rearrangement, or if it was even cancerous at all. It could have been a fungus, or something else as benign. It may or may not have been related to my original lung cancer. Nothing could be certain until a biopsy was done, but a biopsy could not be done until this nodule reached at least 10 millimeters in size. It was still too small.

"What do you suggest we do?" I asked.

"Let's just monitor this," he said, adding that he believed waiting for a biopsy was likely the best course of action.

I normally agree that sometimes the best step forward is to do nothing. Taking an unnecessary action could lead to complications, as any invasive procedure such as surgery or a biopsy comes with risks. But I also thought back to what I read in Hamilton Jordan's book, *No Such Thing As A Bad Day*. That a cancer patient should be vigilant and brave and aggressive in dealing with cancer. Or even what might possibly be cancer.

Patience has never been one of my virtues. I am restless. I want to know things, and I don't like to wait. I had a conversation with Cousin Paul, who suggested I talk directly with a surgeon. He said that while a 7-millimeter nodule was indeed small, it might actually be removable. He told me some surgeons might be reluctant to try and perform surgery in a case like this, but also derided them as being on the wimpy side. He pointed out to me that a highly skilled surgeon might not have a problem with removing something small, and that some people were simply better at surgery than others. I loved hearing doctors trash-talk each other.

Paul told me about a well-regarded thoracic surgeon in the San Fernando Valley named Tyler Green. He had done a residency at Lennox Hill Hospital in New York, where Paul had his practice. I met with Dr. Green, and while he was young, he struck me as sharp. He told me he wanted to have his radiologist look at my case and weigh in on whether a biopsy or surgery was possible. He also suggested targeted radiation was an option if surgery or a biopsy had to wait.

I mentioned this to Dr. Formal who checked out Dr. Green and seemed impressed with his background. But then he noticed something else. Dr. Green was partners with Dr. Bumstead, the surgeon who I had met a decade earlier. Dr. Bumstead was the one whose theory that a pleurodesis could cure cancer was later debunked by every other doctor I spoke with. Dr. Formal said that if I decided to go forward and use Dr. Green to do the surgery, I should make sure he was not traveling in the weeks following the procedure, as that would mean Dr. Bumstead would potentially be covering for him. He added that he would never send a family member to see Dr. Bumstead, which is a huge red flag.

When one doctor does not respect another doctor, they are normally diplomatic, gently suggesting patients look elsewhere for a specialist. They rarely say they would never send family members to see them. But my dealings with Dr. Green never went any further, as he never called me back with his radiologist's opinion. While Dr. Green may have been a good surgeon, his association with Dr. Bumstead left me wondering about his decision-making ability. My gut told me not to follow up with him. Sometimes things just don't feel right, and I've learned to trust my hunches.

I wasn't sure how many thoracic surgeons there were in Los Angeles, but I was sure it was a finite number. At this point, I decided to go back and talk with Dr. Robert McKenna, the surgeon who successfully did my pleurodesis in 2012. After seeing my CT scans, Dr. McKenna said the nodule was indeed small, but he thought it would be very possible for him to remove it via surgery. He told me it would likely require a one or two-night hospital stay.

I pushed him to provide an opinion as to whether he thought this was a regrowth of my original lung cancer, or possibly something benign. He confirmed there was no way to tell without removing it or doing a biopsy. I threw enough questions at him to wear him down, and he finally told me if he had to make a guess, given my past history and the fact that this nodule was indeed growing over time, it might well be stage 1 lung cancer. He also mentioned that I could always do targeted radiation. That would be fairly easy, but surgery was more effective at preventing a recurrence of cancer. My own inexpert opinion was that if we were going to go to all this trouble to look inside my lung, removing this thing surgically sounded like a better plan.

So armed with this new information, I returned to Dr. Formal the following week, to review everything before scheduling surgery. I waited a good 90 minutes in the patient room before he came in. At one point, I told his assistant I was going home, but she implored me to stay, that the doctor was headed to see me right then. He arrived about 15 minutes later and offered no apology for keeping me waiting. He quietly looked over my file, and then said something surprising.

"Well, I've spoken with Dr. McKenna, and it looks like we're all in agreement. We should wait on doing anything."

My jaw dropped. That was clearly not what I was told. But according to Dr. Formal, Dr. McKenna had looked further into my case after I left his office, and he noted the nodule was very close to where I had had my pleurodesis done. What that meant was a fairly routine 30-minute procedure would turn into a not-so-routine 90-minute procedure, and had greater risk. Neither Dr. McKenna nor Dr. Formal recommended surgery at this time, and even a needle biopsy would be a little challenging.

Much earlier in my treatment, I heard about something called a liquid biopsy. This was nothing more than a blood test, one that could not only identify cancer in the body but could provide insight as to what the genetic mutation might be. I had asked Dr. Formal about it at the time, and he did not give it much credence. I brought it up again, but all of a sudden, he was effusive in praising it. Apparently, he had gone to a conference a few months back, where liquid biopsies were being hailed as the next big thing. There was a test called the Guardant 360, and he heartily recommended I do it. He had a phlebotomist come in and draw my blood, and he said they would have results in 7 days.

Being a proactive, heavily involved patient, I waited the 7 days and promptly called for my results. The assistant for Dr. Formal said the results had not come in yet. I summed up the fortitude to wait another 7 days and when I phoned his assistant again, I was told the exact same thing. No results yet. Another 7 days and I received the same uninspired answer. Not yet.

Finally, I asked Cousin Paul if there was a way for me to contact Guardant directly, and he found a phone number for me to call. I got through to someone there and asked when the results of my 360 test would be ready. They looked into my charts and told me the results had been sent to Dr. Formal two weeks earlier. I asked the Guardant phone rep if they could send me a copy of the test results directly, and they emailed it to me right away. I read the report and learned I had tested positive for a new mutation called IDH1, and that an oral treatment was available, meaning I could take a pill for this, if necessary. I called Dr. Formal's office twice to speak with him about it. He did not call me back either time.

We all know doctors are busy people who have to manage their time efficiently, prioritizing patients who have pressing needs, and who may require fast treatment. At that point, one could easily say I was a patient who did not need a prompt response. Any course of action could likely wait a few weeks. But therein lies one of the reasons I believe I have survived more than 10 years with a deadly disease. I don't wait around for things to gather steam. I'm proactive. And I expect those treating me to be proactive, too.

I thought back to my time with Dr. Lieber, and with his excellent assistant Jorge Munoz, who would always get back to me quickly. I knew I was lucky to have them, but I didn't realize just how lucky I had been until I was faced with staff who were not responsive at all. My case might be low priority for the doctor, but it was very much high priority for me. Doctors care for many patients; I only have one patient to look out for. And I make sure my one patient's needs are met.

So, what do you do when your doctor does not call you back? Lots of thoughts entered my mind, and none of them were good. Was he traveling? Was he ill? Had I asked him too many questions at our meetings? Was his assistant not giving him my messages? I wanted to make a decision on what to do next, and I had no way to contact Dr. Formal other than going through his assistant, which was leading me nowhere. Unlike Dr. Lieber, I did not have Dr. Formal's personal cell phone number, and I certainly did not have his wife's cell phone number. I felt like a teenage boy whose girlfriend was telegraphing some not-so-subtle signals she would be breaking up with him soon. But I wasn't a teenage boy, and I wasn't about to be ghosted.

I thought back to when Dr. Lieber retired, and he had mentioned a lung cancer specialist at the clinic, Dr. Ani Balmanoukian. I called her assistant and set up an appointment to meet this new oncologist the next day. She was a good bit younger than Dr. Formal and Dr. Lieber, but she seemed bright and personable and liked to go by Dr. Annie. And she had not only looked into my file, but she had called Dr. Ou to find out more about me. Not only did Dr. Ou remember me, but he remembered I had written numerous books, that Matthew had gone to college at his alma mater, Berkeley, and that we had just gotten back from a trip to New Orleans. Dr. Annie seemed very interested in the situation with my new nodule, and her mind moved as quickly as Dr. Lieber's. I liked that.

She looked at the Guardant 360 report and noted right away that the IDH1 mutation was rarely associated with lung cancer. It was more typically related to leukemia; this was a little unsettling, but there were only traces of it. We discussed the situation and she understood my desire to not wait for the nodule to keep growing until a biopsy could be done. We were clearly on the same wavelength. We were connecting. So at the end of our session, I popped the question. Would she like to be my primary oncologist? She was a little taken aback, and apparently there is a protocol for a patient switching doctors within the same clinic. She asked if I wouldn't mind talking to Dr. Formal about it. I said sure. I just wasn't so certain he'd return my calls.

Later that day, my phone buzzed, and I saw it was *Dr. Formal calling me*. We had a pleasant chat, I did not chastise him for not returning any of my calls, or for not following up on the Guardant 360, or for being completely unreachable for weeks. I did not tell him what happened with his assistant, figuring it wasn't my role to manage his staff. I also didn't want to get anyone fired. But I mostly wanted to move on. Our conversation, like most of the ones I had with Dr. Formal, was long. He mentioned I was an "interesting" patient, and one could take that many ways. I finally laid out what I thought were my options. I spoke calmly, but I was starting to seethe. I didn't mind owning my cancer, but it felt like I was becoming my own oncologist here.

"It looks like surgery is not a good option for me," I said. "And even if we were able to do a biopsy, what do we do with that information? The nodule is growing slowly, and since the liquid biopsy did not indicate there was ROS1 in my system, there's a good probability that the Crizotinib is still working. So I'm obviously not going to stop taking Crizotinib. And even if a biopsy tells us this nodule has a different genetic mutation, I don't think I can take two TKIs at the same time. That leaves me with two options. Do targeted radiation, or do nothing."

There was a long pause before he finally spoke. "I think doing targeted radiation is a reasonable choice."

He provided me with the name of a good radiation oncologist. He told me what to expect. And at that point, near the end of our call, I began to initiate our breakup.

"You know," I said, "given the fact that I'm an interesting, or perhaps, unusual patient, do you think it might be better off if I were to see a lung cancer specialist? Maybe someone like Dr. Balmanoukian?"

There was another pause, but he quickly recovered and agreed. Maybe it was better this way. He said that, of course, the change made sense, that he was trained to be a generalist, but a lung cancer specialist might indeed be better for me. He asked if I would stay in touch and let him know how I was doing, because he was still interested in my situation. I agreed, although I suspected we would never speak again. And so Dr. Formal and I parted, in an amicable way, and in the way certain relationships end. The way partners separate when a relationship has run its course, even if the course was brief. There wasn't any acrimony, and there wasn't any blame. It ended, not with a bang, but with a whimper. It ended with politeness and without any finger-pointing. It ended with someone telling a white lie to spare the other person's feelings. It ended with someone saying, "No, it's not you. It's me."

25

The High Cost Of Living

The process of removing a nodule is sometimes called "weeding the garden." Taking this simile a little further, chemo is like spraying the entire garden with weed killer, which means it will likely kill both weeds and healthy plants indiscriminately. Surgery is akin to yanking out clumps of weeds, which can also take out the soil around them. But targeted radiation is more like isolating the weeds, zapping them, and leaving them to wither and die without disturbing anything else in the garden. The downside, however, is that new weeds are more likely to grow back at some point.

The radiation oncologist at St. John's hospital was a friendly guy, and he clearly explained what I could expect. Targeted radiation doesn't kill the cancer cells on contact; rather, it slows the nodule's growth by damaging its DNA. I would be strapped to a gurney for about 20 minutes, while they sent beams of radiation directly onto the nodule in my lung. They would do 5 sessions over a period of 10 days. I did not need to do anything to prepare. He told me it was simple and straightforward.

So every other day I drove to the hospital, always parking at a meter a few blocks away to avoid the $18 parking fee at St. John's. The radiation room was spacious and dark, and reminded me of the narrow area in Disneyland where you first walk inside Space Mountain. It felt very modern. The technicians strapped me in so tight I could hardly breathe, solely to prevent movement, and ensure the targeted radiation could, well, hit its target. I asked where the radiation oncologist was, and one of the technicians laughed.

"Oh, rest assured, you don't want him doing this," he smiled. "But he's monitoring things."

Somehow that did not make me feel either rested or assured, but after 10 years of living with cancer, I knew you sometimes have to take things as they come. The 5 radiation treatments were painless, albeit a little uncomfortable. A few months later, we did CT scans, and the 7-millimeter nodule had shrunk to 4 millimeters, and Dr. Annie said if it was cancer, it would now likely be gone.

"Because we didn't do a biopsy, we can't know for certain that this was cancer," she told me and added that the thing formerly known as a nodule now looked more like scar tissue.

One more problem solved, or at least put off for a while. There was always a chance of recurrence, but that would be another worry for another day. In my world, there was always some problem springing up.

But a big reason for doing radiation was so I could continue taking Crizotinib. The goal of many lung cancer patients is to simply extend their runway on each drug, for as long as possible. To try and stick around long enough for the next big treatment to be discovered. For the next promising clinical trial to open.

Therein was the big concern for me. Clinical trials often want patients who have been on no more than a few drugs. They don't want results of the trial impacted by the patient who has developed a resistance to certain medications, which may not reflect the efficacy of the new drug. But also, there are only a limited number of drugs available that can work on patients, and we try to maximize our time on these – to obviously maximize our survival time overall.

When the trial for Crizotinib ended, I began getting the drug through a standard prescription, with my health insurance company picking up the lion's share of the cost. Since Pfizer waived my co-pay, I had been paying nothing for Crizotinib since 2012. But then I turned 65 at the end of 2021, and I entered into the world of Medicare. The rules suddenly changed.

At the start of 2022, I contacted Pfizer to apply for a new co-pay waiver, assuming it would be a simple process. I assumed wrong. My application was rejected. As I was still working, my income exceeded the threshold they established for waiving the co-pay for Medicare recipients. So my co-pay, the out-of-pocket price I would pay to continue to receive this drug, would increase from $0 to $16,000 a year.

The reason for this situation is a little complex. The retail price established for Crizotinib is $20,481 per month, or $245,772 per year. Yes, almost a quarter of a million dollars annually. Drug companies like to point out that these hefty prices help cover the cost of developing the many drugs that fail to get positive results in the lab. How much of this is true is conjecture, since private companies only release so much information about their business practices.

Medicare rules in 2022 stated that once a patient has paid roughly $7,000 out of their own pockets, catastrophic coverage starts, and Medicare will then cover 95 percent of the cost of the drug. That sounds nice. But with Crizotinib's monthly cost being over $20,000, my portion would be over $1,000 a month. At that time, there was no cap on a patient's maximum out-of-pocket cost, so while Medicare would pay most of the expense, my portion would be significant. A new law was passed by Congress later that year which capped patients' out-of-pocket drug cost at $2,000 annually. Unfortunately, that part of the new law does not fully kick in until 2025.

Part of the problem is the way in which Medicare's thorny rules were originally written. Medicare was, by law, not allowed to negotiate prescription drug prices with pharmaceutical companies. The pharmaceutical companies can set their prices as high as the market will bear. The government has no choice but to cover medications at whatever price a drug company sets. As such, Medicare is not eligible to get a discount. They pay retail. The new 2022 law does allow Medicare to begin negotiating the price of prescription drugs, but only for a very limited number of them at first. By 2030, more drugs will be included in Medicare's ability to negotiate prices, but it is unclear whether Crizotinib will be one of them.

When my co-pay waiver application was rejected, Pfizer immediately invited me to appeal this decision – through the same department that just rejected the application I'd just sent in. It was on me to provide evidence that my family's expenses were high enough for the company to justify a new waiver. I thought it a little absurd to appeal to the same department that initially rejected my application, but having worked in the corporate world, I understood bureaucracies. I filled out the forms and waited for a decision.

I am of two minds when it comes to drug companies. I am eternally grateful to Pfizer for developing this drug. Without Crizotinib, it is unlikely I would have survived lung cancer for over ten years following my 2012 diagnosis. For me, Crizotinib was a miracle drug, and the extra time has been precious beyond words. I was able to see Matthew's high school basketball games, see him graduate from college, and I was able to reach my dream career as a novelist. But transitioning to Medicare threw a financial wrench into my semi-blissful experience. The cost of Crizotinib is extremely high, and even with Medicare and the best drug coverage available, my co-pay would suddenly become extremely high as well. Pharmaceutical companies are not altruistic; these pricey drugs designed to manage long-term conditions are also designed to secure highly profitable long-term customers.

While I was trying to find a solution to all this, our insurance broker took us through our options for getting Medicare Plan D drug coverage. All of the plans had very steep co-pays, and there were no good alternatives. We explored getting assistance through charitable organizations, but I did not qualify financially because I was still working. I could have stayed on the private insurance plan I had before Medicare, but that cost more than $20,000 a year in premiums alone, which did not make it a viable choice. The money we saved by going onto Medicare would now be offset by the money going toward co-pays for Crizotinib.

At some point, I will stop working, and my income then may more easily qualify me for Pfizer's Patient Assistance Program. Or, at some point, Crizotinib might stop working for me, and I'll need to move on to another treatment. I'm not looking forward to either scenario, but the good part about working is that I'll be able to put aside money to pay for Crizotinib. There is no other option. For me, Crizotinib is a little like insulin is for a diabetic patient. I need it to live. I'll pay whatever. Thankfully I won't have to pay the full $20,000 a month, because, like most people, we would run out of money very fast.

About a month after I sent in my appeal to Pfizer, there was a knock at my door. The UPS delivery guy handed me a small package in an unmarked envelope with a return address somewhere in South Dakota. When I opened it up, there was a one-month supply of Crizotinib. I read the mouse print on the label on the bottle and finally saw that the medication was fulfilled by Pfizer's Patient Assistance Program. I did not receive a letter about this until a week later, which confirmed that my appeal had been approved. Corporations sometimes work in mysterious ways, and sometimes they do good. This was one of those times.

26

Enter Stage 5

I am one of those people who beat the odds. At the time of my diagnosis in 2012, the five-year life expectancy for stage 4 lung cancer patients was under 10 percent. I have become one of *those guys*. I managed to reach stage 5.

I believe I am still here because of good luck and good decisions, and frankly, I needed both. I could not have survived with only one of these, and not the other. Had I been diagnosed with this type of lung cancer just two years earlier, doctors would have been unaware Crizotinib might be effective for me. Had I been diagnosed a few years later, the trial might have been closed. I was unlucky to be a non-smoker getting lung cancer, but incredibly lucky for the timing to occur when it did.

I've heard a few definitions of luck, and I'll share a couple of them here. The English poet, John Milton, once said "luck is the residue of design," although Branch Rickey popularized that when he ran the Brooklyn Dodgers almost a century ago. A fortune cookie I once opened told me "luck is where preparation meets opportunity." Both sayings get to the same idea, which is you put yourself in a position to have good luck. You talk to smart people. You make good decisions. When faced with a choice of continuing on chemotherapy or entering a clinical trial, I chose the trial. It sounds like an easy decision now. A decade ago, it was not.

Life is not fair, and it will probably never be fair. Some people seem to get many breaks, while others are forced to endure many hardships. This is especially true in the cancer world. There is no good explanation for why Crizotinib worked so well for so long on me – but not as well on others. There is no good reason why my diagnosis happened just as a clinical trial was opening up close to our home, which provided me with the right drug at the right time, and at a convenient location. My only requirement was going in for regular scans and blood tests, a fairly easy protocol.

Call it what you will, be it fate, be it divine intervention, be it something else entirely, but if I had to have been stricken with terminal lung cancer, I could not have scripted it any better. Had I been diagnosed at age 35 instead of age 55, I'm sure I would have been less accepting of what life handed me. My career did not take off until my mid-30s, and it was only then that I met Andrea and we had Matthew shortly thereafter. Had I been diagnosed around that time – as certain lung cancer patients have – I'm sure I would have felt I had missed an important aspect of life. That it happened at age 55 allowed me to have success in building both my career and my personal life. Perhaps this extra time was also afforded to me so I could grow as an author and write this book and to share my experiences, in the hope that others could somehow benefit from what I've learned. None of this can be validated, though. It is all speculation. Life's meanings are complex. They are often revealed by how you perceive them.

To be honest, though, there are a few things I did to achieve a better outcome. Going to the doctor immediately when I felt back pain arose was irrefutably the best thing I'd ever done for myself. There is no substitute for early detection of cancer. When caught at the initial stages, there are far more options for a good outcome. Although my cancer had spread to other parts of the body before the warning sign of back pain emerged, the fact that Dr. Gordon sent me in for a chest X-ray right away allowed us to identify a lung tumor quickly. Within just 6 weeks, the tumor had grown by almost 50 percent, so beginning chemotherapy right away had been crucial to halting progression of the disease.

As to choosing the correct treatment, there was no surefire blueprint for success. Seeking out good doctors and asking for their opinions is a given. But as I discovered, some doctors have their own unproven theories, which means confirming or debunking these with other doctors. This is clearly the most challenging part to navigate. Andrea went with me to a lot of doctor appointments; bringing along a family member can be helpful. In addition to conjuring up pertinent questions you might not have thought of, they can also help you remember details the doctor relayed during your appointment. Patients frequently have so many things on our minds that having someone at your side can be an enormous help.

Certain aspects of my good fortune are admittedly uncontrollable on the surface. Having a number of cousins who were not just doctors, but oncologists, was incredibly lucky. But I also peppered them with a lot of questions, and more importantly, listened to their advice. People can't help you unless you allow them to. The CEO of a company is not always the smartest guy in the office. But successful CEOs hire and retain smart people, and pay attention to what they have to say.

A friend once hypothesized that my financial worries a few years before might have contributed to the cancer emerging when it did. I had heard this before and had observed some interesting stories. A woman whose fiancée suddenly broke off their engagement was diagnosed with breast cancer a few months later. A man who was involved in a serious bicycle accident was diagnosed with colon cancer shortly afterward. Is there a connection between one awful event and a cancer diagnosis that soon followed? There's no way we can be certain about this type of cause and effect. But it can give you pause. There are just so many things we don't know yet.

My future is uncertain, just as everyone's future is uncertain. As I was finishing this book, a routine blood test during my annual physical showed high PSA levels. I went in for an MRI of the prostate and it revealed a 2-centimeter lesion. I will soon have it biopsied, and if it's cancer, I'll explore treatment options. And pray. And ask questions of as many doctors who will listen to me. I briefly thought of not going forward with publishing this book until I knew more about this lesion. But Matthew reminded me that I had wanted to write this book to serve as a guide and an inspiration for people who were newly diagnosed with cancer. I just never dreamed that could be me again. You never know.

One thing I do know for certain though is that our longevity can turn on a dime. My experience long ago, taking the flight from Chicago to Pittsburgh, the one that did not result in a horrible crash, taught me about the randomness of life. So did my brother's fatal car accident. We aren't aware of what's in store for us. In 2012, I had no idea that I'd still be on Crizotinib over a decade later. I also did not know that my short-term consulting gig at Herbalife would last for many years, instead of a few short months. But I did know that I wanted to live as normal a life as I could for as long as I could. That was my mission. So far, I've managed to achieve that.

I've put together a list of things cancer patients can do to help themselves. I call it the "Top 10 Habits of Highly Successful Cancer Patients." It is not an exhaustive list, rather, it includes some of the ideas and practices that have worked for me. Maybe they can work for you, or someone you care about. You don't know until you try.

The Top 10 Habits of Highly Successful Cancer Patients

1. Establish Your Goals

Your goal can be anything. It can be to live until you're 100. It can be to only live without pain. For me, it was to live as normal a life as I could, for as long as I could. It's important to understand what it is you really want, because many treatment decisions will stem from that. Knowing what your goals are will help you decide how risky or painful the treatments you undergo should be. If your goal is indeed to live to 100, you'll be open to aggressive procedures, but these may bring complications with them. Remember, there is no one right or wrong answer here, only the one that is right for you.

2. Ask Questions

Do not be afraid to ask questions. Make lists of questions you have before you go in for your doctor's appointment, so you won't forget anything. Don't be afraid to ask whatever questions are on your mind; there are no dumb questions here. You need to understand as much as you can about your treatment options and how they will affect you. Don't worry about what a doctor or a nurse might think of you for asking these. You're not there to impress them. You're there to find the right path toward achieving your goals, whatever those goals happen to be. You can ask the doctor what they recommend, but remember, the doctors are just giving you their opinion. An informed opinion for sure, but remember that is still just their point of view.

3. Get Second Opinions

No one has perfect knowledge; doctors are human and they can make mistakes. It's important to confirm that your doctor's recommendation is reasonably in line with what other doctors recommend also, or at least not wildly differing from standard protocol – unless you're comfortable with a high level of risk. Some doctors have their pet theories about various treatments; they might be right, but these theories may be unproven, and they may be wrong. You'll have to decide if you want to roll the dice when one doctor's judgment goes against what the other doctors are recommending. I'm not saying don't do it. But if you do, go into it with your eyes open.

And don't be concerned about insulting a doctor by telling them you'd like a second opinion. Any doctor who takes offense at this standard step should be viewed with extreme caution. If a doctor tells you something that doesn't sound right, run it by another doctor. If you don't feel as if you're getting the best possible care, switch doctors. And if you live in a small community where there are not a lot of doctors, consider traveling to consult with someone else. In extreme cases, you may even want to think about moving to a community with better health care services.

4. Take Calculated Risks

Sometimes doctors disagree on treatments. Medicine can be as much an art as it is a science. There may be new treatments that are not yet established as standard protocol, but you and your doctor might decide this is right for you. Clarify what a new treatment offers, what the side effects are, and what the likelihood of a successful outcome might be. If the standard treatment doesn't appear to provide you with what you need, and a new treatment offers more hope, the new one is worth considering. In dealing with cancer, you face an enemy that is very clever. Cancer cells can adapt and change in ways that can frustrate treatment. Sometimes trying a new treatment is the best move forward. You may not understand all the science behind it, but just be sure you understand the pros and cons that come with a new option.

5. Use the Internet – Don't Let It Use You

The internet can truly be a wonderful source of information, but it can also be a source of outdated, incorrect, and even dishonest content. Answers you find on the internet should be verified before you go forward with making decisions on your treatment. You can explore various cancer forums, but remember, you are typically seeing the views of other patients, not doctors. These experiences can be quite helpful, but what you learn there should not be considered gospel. They can provide the stimulus for questions you should ask your doctor to confirm.

6. Connect With Other Patients

As much as friends and family are supportive, no one can truly understand what you're going through like another cancer patient can. The types of fears and anxieties patients experience are not uncommon; others go through them, too. It's helpful to be able to talk about these issues with someone enduring the same experience – or one who has already gone through it and help you move forward.

7. Seek Financial Help

If you are having trouble paying doctor or hospital bills, or if the medication you need is too expensive, there are charitable organizations that can provide assistance. They will usually require seeing your financial records and tax statements, but this is often worth pursuing. Some people have had success in starting Go Fund Me campaigns. No one should stop medical care strictly because of finances. There are often options out there. You can ask your doctor, ask the drug manufacturer, ask your friends or family, ask people who are in your religious organization, or join an internet support group and ask other patients. It never hurts to try.

8. Make Yourself the CEO of Your Cancer

A CEO is the Chief Executive Officer, the person who is in charge. You are in charge of your own cancer. Doctors mean well and want to help, but you will be the one living with the ramifications of these treatment decisions, not them. Good decisions can extend your life, poor decisions can shorten your life. Make sure you're the one who gives the final okay, or at least approves the treatment your doctor recommends. Don't be afraid to question or to say no to treatments you don't understand, or ones that make you feel uncomfortable. Ultimately, it's your life. You need to be in charge of it. Your primary concern should be about you.

9. Forgive Yourself

My father-in-law used to say, "Be good to yourself." We often beat ourselves up emotionally for things we did or didn't do. You can't change the past, but you can be more accepting of your decisions. Forgive yourself for your previous mistakes. We're all human. We're all imperfect. We may have made some poor decisions in the past, but that's in the past. If you had that 2nd slice of cake or that 3rd glass of wine or said the wrong thing at the wrong time, be aware that no one else should sit in judgment of you. Not even you.

10. Be Brave

It is natural to be fearful and anxious when you've been diagnosed with a deadly disease. It is important to get those feelings out with someone who can sympathize with what you're going through. But try hard to focus on a positive outcome, and believe that you can overcome your challenges. As Dr. Lieber taught me, a positive outlook will afford you a better quality of life, regardless of what happens with your treatment. And here's a little secret. If you don't think you can be brave, you can act like you are. Pretend. It's not that hard. No one will know the difference.

Acknowledgements

I owe so much to so many people, I doubt I could name all of them. But I will name some.

To Earl Gordon, Daniel Lieber, and Ignatius Ou, I owe you my life. You are all brilliant doctors – and even better human beings.

To my oncologist cousins, Paul Baron and Steve Neudorf, I cannot thank you enough for graciously indulging me with your time and knowledge, and patiently explaining the many aspects of cancer in both fine detail and in ways I could understand.

To Ani Balmanoukian and Jessica Finley, for picking up the heavy batons that Dr. Lieber and Dr. Gordon handed you, and showing me that I am still in very good hands.

To Jorge Munoz, who served as Dr. Lieber's assistant. You demonstrate what every medical office employee should be. Diligent, compassionate, and extraordinarily good at your job.

To Michele Azada and Oliver Quinones and the team at the Chao Cancer Center at UC-Irvine, thank you for your caring, your efforts, and for always being on top of things.

To the crew at Pfizer (you know who you are), thank you for all of your hard work.

To those who regularly checked in with me and boosted my spirits, you embody what friendship is. That's you, Jan and Greg Martin, Lisa Yates, Tara Cathcart, Andy Erman, Mary Walsh, Michael Meltzer, Larry Mazin, Howard Domfort, Bob Hollies, Ron Rabatsky, Crystal Lofink, Rick DeLoia, Dave Fruchtman, Rachel Parker, Terry Ferguson, Dan Schechter, Steve Miller, Joanne Baker, Karen and Brent Byrd.

To my doctor friends and relatives who provided much-needed advice and guidance, I'd like to thank Craig Pursuit, Bill Parker, Allen Weiner, Norman Friedman, and Lisa Baron.

To my family and extended family who have always been there for lots of moral support and encouragement, my many cousins and in-laws, your support and caring have been essential. You define what family is all about. Bennett Lieberman, Cherie and John Ahearn, Rita and Bridget Lieberman, Diana Steinman, Judy and Robert Liebross, the Neudorf clan, the Baron clan, Jane and Bob Gerstein, Keren and Jim Lieberman, the Rubins, Lucy and Tom Sponsler, Enid and Richard Graddis, Barbara Cahn, and oh heck, the entire Lieberman clan.

To Lynn Balsamo for picking up the gauntlet, reading my books and making great suggestions, and being a wonderful and compassionate friend.

To the friends and relatives who did not get past their cancer diagnosis, there are too many to name, but I'll list a few: Allen Fremont, Jane Conaway, Andrea Hopmeyer, Marilynn Lieberman, Brad Burlingame, Craig Uthe, Colleen McHorney, Fred Zufryden, Jim Lieberman, Steve Lieberman, and Rajeana Jensen.

To Jen Gorman, for laughing at my jokes, maintaining your equilibrium, and handling the unfathomable with grace, maturity, and intelligence.

And finally to my dear wife Andrea, and to my marvelous son Matthew. You have made me a better person. You are simply the best. I love you so much.

Made in the USA
Columbia, SC
03 October 2023

23780133R00133